SACRED VOICES

of the Nyingma Masters

SACRED VOICES

of the Nyingma Masters

Photographed and compiled by Sandra Scales

Written and edited by Kathryn Meeske and Sandra Scales

PADMA PUBLISHING

For my son, Noah, with thanks for his loving support.

Published by Padma Publishing
P.O. Box 279
Junction City, California 96048-0279

© Sandra Scales 2004

Printed in Italy by
Editoriale Bortolazzi-Stei (EBS)
First Printing

Library of Congress
Cataloging-in-Publication Data

Scales, Sandra
Sacred voices of the Nyingma masters /
Sandra Scales. — 1ST ED.
p. cm.
ISBN 1-881847-35-7 (alk. paper)
1. Rñiṇ-ma-pa (Sect)—Doctrines. 1.
Title.

BQ7662.4.S325   2004
294.3'923'0922—DC22
2003027348

Individuals other than those to whom chapters
are devoted: Dudjom Yangsi Pema Ösel Rinpoche,
pages 243 and 245; Khyentse Yangsi Rinpoche,
page 248; Khandro Damchö and Melitis Kwong,
page 97; Semo Sonam Palmo and Semo Tseyang
Palmo, page 167; Khandro Pema Dechen, page 57

Calligraphy by Dzongsar Khyentse Rinpoche.

Bodhgaya Buddha photograph on page 6 courtesy
of Tulku Pema Rinpoche. Photograph of Mindroling
Rinpoche on page 41 courtesy of Lama Ripa.

SACRED VOICES was designed by Joseph Guglietti.
It was composed on a Macintosh computer using
Sabon, Monotype Bembo and Trajan.

The photographs were taken with a Leica M3,
using Kodak Tri-X pan 400 film. The scans and
digital preparation were done in collaboration
with Dennis Hearne.

Author's Note

THIS BOOK BEGAN BECAUSE OF THE EVER-PRESENT KINDNESS OF KYABJE DUDJOM RINPOCHE. The Dudjom Tersar initiations given by Kyabje Rinpoche in 1977 drew many of the Nyingmapas together in the Kathmandu Valley. The lightness and majesty of their combined presence was both magical and humbling; however, after that auspicious occasion, I myself never had the opportunity to see them together in one place. This is what inspired me to request permission from Kyabje Rinpoche to compile the teachings and images of some of the Nyingma masters whom I had met over time. After I made the request, Kyabje Rinpoche wrote a letter of encouragement for the project, which I then showed to the Nyingma lamas whose oral instructions and images are the heart of *Sacred Voices*. In requesting the teachings included here, I tried to follow the course of Kyabje Dudjom Rinpoche's blessings. It must be clearly stated that this book is in no way a complete representation of the many great Nyingmapas who bless this earth, or the innumerable ways in which their words and actions guide beings on the spiritual path.

In Tibetan Buddhism, oral instruction is a central process whereby teachings are given in response to the particular needs of individuals or groups. Hence, trusting the wisdom of these esteemed masters, I asked them to give teachings they thought most appropriate for readers of this book. Each teaching is preceded by a section recounting my meetings with these rinpoches. While any description of the revered holders of the lineage cannot begin to capture the radiance of their being, it was my hope that including this additional element might further transport the reader to the sphere of the Nyingmapas. The content of the preambles is true only to my own perceptions, and some will find them unnecessary reading.

The teachings were taped, transcribed and edited, then returned to the masters for final approval. The chapters have been edited with the good but perhaps poorly executed intention of maintaining the authentic tone and unique speaking style of each rinpoche. This includes using punctuation that corresponds with the emphasis and pauses in their speech, as well as mine in the preambles. The work of this book is humbly offered to the teachers whose words grace these pages. We maladroit writers have doubtless made mistakes in the text; for those who open this book, may the pristine words of the masters render all errors free of consequence.

ALL ROYALTIES FROM THIS BOOK WILL BE DONATED TO THE SAVING OF LIVES AS explained in Chadral Sangye Dorje Rinpoche's teaching. The practice of saving lives can be a joyful experience. Children in particular seem to take great delight in rescuing animals, and for many individuals, families and dharma communities, this practice provides a relatively simple and tangible, yet profound way of expressing compassion. There are numerous ways to save the lives of beings. Some of the animals that can be purchased and released are saltwater baitfish from ocean docks, as well as feeder fish, worms and crickets from pet stores. For those with the appropriate land, larger animals such as chickens and cows destined for slaughter can also be purchased. Dogs, cats and other animals can be adopted from shelters where they would otherwise be put to sleep. When releasing the animals, one can offer one's own good wishes or recite prayers written specifically for this purpose. Various Buddhist centers also perform this practice regularly and welcome participation. More information about the practice of ransoming and saving lives can be found at www.saving-lives.net.

To Prince Siddhartha of the Shakyas, without whom the
lamp of the path beyond extremes would not be lit;

To Vidyadhara Prahevajra, acharya Padmasambhava of
Oddiyana, mahapandita Vimalamitra and yogi Shri Simha,
and the other pioneers who brightened this light;

To Bhikshu Shantarakshita, dharma king Trisong of Tibet,
lady Tsogyal, translator Vairochana and many others who
illuminated Tibet with this torch;

To Nyima Öser of Nyang, Guru Chowang, peerless
Longchenpa and Rongzompa, the poet Jigme Lingpa, along
with numerous treasure revealers, scholars and saints who
preserved the teachings;

To the Great Fifth Dalai Lama Lobsang Gyatso, Vajra Master
Terdak Lingpa, Khyentse Wangpo and Kongtrul Lodrö Thaye,
Chokgyur Lingpa, Paltrul of Dza and Mipham of Ju, who
propagated the dharma;

To fearless Jigdral Yeshe Dorje and omniscient Tashi Paljor
and our root gurus without whose kindness our eyes would
not be opened to the dharma;

With fervent devotion—born of reason and understanding—
we supplicate you. May we be liberated from the darkness
by just seeing your face or hearing your name.

May the great tradition of Khenpo Shantarakshita, Lopön Padmasambhava

and Dharma King Trisong Deutsen

Increase and spread throughout the three realms.

May the appearance of the Three Jewels and the mindstreams of beings remain inseparable,

And bring sublime well-being throughout the three times.

CONTENTS

INTRODUCTION

FOR MORE THAN A THOUSAND YEARS, Tibetan bells have echoed across the Himalayan mountain range, the sounds of a culture rich with compassion, resilience and courage. The strength of the Tibetan people is forged from the words of Lord Buddha, the great champion of compassion. His teachings are the foundation of the entire Tibetan community. With the Communist invasion of Tibet, these nonviolent people were forced to scatter across neighboring countries, bringing their woolen robes and faith to the dusty heat of India and the terraced rice fields of Nepal. The battle the Tibetans have won is that of maintaining their Buddhist faith even in the face of devastating brutality. In this, they are the victors.

The original school of Tibetan Buddhism blossomed centuries ago in the high mountains and wind-chilled plains of Tibet. The lineage remains intact and vibrant today. The ambassadors of this tradition are now known as the Nyingmapas, the Ancient Ones. They are teachers, scholars, saints and siddhas who embody an indestructible wisdom; astute specialists, they are masters of the very nature of mind, not merely outer circumstances. These masters teach us how to transform our own obdurate tendencies—to help both ourselves and others navigate sorrows and increase happiness, ultimately leading beings to enlightenment. They are, however, nomads at heart, and to find them gathered in one location is a rare occurrence. This peripatetic leaning is a reflection of the wish to help as many beings as possible, and stems in part from the genesis of what has come to be known as Nyingma, the Ancient Translation School.

The Nyingma holds the complete, unadulterated Buddhist teachings as transmitted by Shantarakshita, Padmasambhava, Vimalamitra and other consummate Indian masters. These exalted beings joined with a hundred illustrious panditas, translating an inestimable number of Sanskrit texts of both sutra and tantra, and saturating Tibet with a vast treasury of knowledge. The accessibility and precise translation of these texts were vital to the spread of Buddhism in Tibet. In this early propagation of the dharma, the teachings were passed on to yogis, yoginis, monks, nuns and laypeople. The Nyingma thus gave rise to a diverse and widespread continuum of teaching and practice, principally associated with six mother monasteries and their numerous branch monasteries. Nourished by the continued discovery of treasure teachings hidden long ago for the benefit of future generations, the tradition thrives in the present time, dispersing the blessings of Padmasambhava to far-flung regions of the world. This fluidity, this quality of timeliness, is inherent in the wisdom and beauty of the Nyingma.

When Dzongsar Khyentse Rinpoche was asked on one occasion to speak about the special qualities of the Nyingmapas, he responded, "Nyingma was the dawn of Buddhism in Tibet, and imparts the blessing of 'openness,' the blessing of being 'carefree.' Rigdzin Jigme Lingpa, one of the greatest Nyingma saints, said, 'At all times and in all circumstances, may the wish to conform to conventional expectations not arise even for an instant. If, due to the power of strong habits, such deluded intentions occur, may they not succeed.' Though inconspicuous, Nyingma emanates a definite steady influence to release individuals and groups from the pain of grasping—not only ideological grasping, but all forms of grasping—the day-to-day and the minute-to-minute."

The masters who hold and transmit the remarkable energy of the Nyingma lineage are still with us, walking on this earth today. Many of the teachers represented in this book are among the last Nyingma Buddhist masters to have received their training in Tibet, and as such, their words and images honor a culture abundant with spiritual wealth. The younger incarnate lamas included here are the spiritual heirs who carry on this unbroken lineage. They may traverse five continents in a matter of weeks, instructing people from vastly diverse societies. The grandfathers, sons and daughters of this tradition reflect the diversity of the Buddhist teachings; their distinct voices form a river of continuity leading to the sea of enlightenment. The value of their collective knowledge speaks for itself. In *Sacred Voices,* the Nyingmapas provide practical methods for keeping our actions congruent with our spiritual aspirations. Through their words, may we also be victorious.

KYABJE DUDJOM RINPOCHE

Meeting

KYABJE DUDJOM RINPOCHE

THIS JOURNEY BEGAN ALMOST BY ACCIDENT—a serendipitous meeting with an esteemed and holy lama changed the course of my life. In 1976 I met Kyabje Dudjom Rinpoche in Berkeley, California. Reverence arose instantaneously. I remember being shocked that someone so sublime could exist in this world. It seemed as though his being was the fulcrum of everything sacred; I had met the Buddha.

The guiding principles of my life changed in that moment, leaving no choice other than to be near this great master, hear his teachings, and try to learn and practice according to his instructions. When Dudjom Rinpoche returned to Nepal, I followed with my two children. Many of our belongings were sold to finance the trip. To give up some antiques, the piano, and even my darkroom equipment for the purpose seemed quite rational at the time. We closed up our house and left for what was intended to be a six-month sojourn in Nepal.

The plane was nearly empty flying to this unfamiliar land, and both the children were seated at windows, anxious to see what awaited them. The formidable Himalayas came into view, surrounding the capital city in a stern embrace. Impossibly green terraces of rice were interspersed with the straw roofs of mud-plastered homes, and my eight-year-old daughter turned from the window briefly to ask if we would be living in a grass hut. The plane banked to the left, and we saw the great Boudhanath stupa, its massive white dome anchoring an expansive, inviting valley. The flight attendant's voice floated through the cabin, "Namaste (the God in me greets the God in you). Welcome to Nepal."

We walked down the steps of the plane and across the tarmac to the single room of the airport terminal to collect our ten bags (a duffel full of diapers, a small satchel containing favorite Barbie dolls, a trunk filled with Legos, and other suitcases packed with far too many clothes). We pushed and dragged our luggage into two taxis and ended up in a $3-per-night room at the Kathmandu Guest House. Within weeks we found a small house for rent near the stupa, and the children quickly acclimated themselves to their new surroundings. Unexpectedly, Kathmandu began to feel like home.

I visited Dudjom Rinpoche as often as possible, seeking his guidance. He was revered as one of the greatest Dzogchen masters and tertons of our modern age and a living representative of Guru Rinpoche himself. Other masters and countless devotees uttered his name with awe and deep respect. Dudjom Rinpoche was both a poet and scholar with encyclopedic knowledge; he wrote, revised and corrected many Buddhist texts, including the whole canon of the Nyingma school. Many lamas from all schools of Tibetan Buddhism traveled great distances to receive teachings from Dudjom Rinpoche. And out of his spontaneous, uninterrupted kindness, Rinpoche also saw unschooled itinerants like myself, who could only begin to intuit the majesty and spiritual authority of Kyabje Dudjom Rinpoche.

Six months passed very quickly in that uncommon environment. Shortly before we were scheduled to return to the United States, we heard that Kyabje Dudjom Rinpoche was to give the Dudjom Tersar initiations in the following months, so we postponed our departure. For Nyingmapas, the initiations were a most rare and precious occurrence. Like thousands of tributaries making their way to the ocean, rinpoches, monks and nuns, yogins and laypersons converged on Kathmandu—cascading from flinty caves in Tibet, the hot plains of India, and the terraced lands of Sikkim, Bhutan and Ladakh. Enormous tents of bleached cotton were erected over the fallow rice paddies surrounding Dudjom Monastery, and each day thousands of people sat shoulder to shoulder listening to His Holiness' gentle intonation. For many weeks, Dudjom Rinpoche recited sacred texts as he gave the entire body of initiations. At the conclusion of the ceremonies, he himself walked through the crowd, holding the ritual implements as he made his way along impromptu aisles formed by hastily shifting bodies. As evening slowly fell, a bright net of stars draped the sky above. It took until the early morning hours for Kyabje Rinpoche to touch each attendee on the head. The moment of his blessing was one of incomparable grace. By the time the initiations were completed, we had decided to make Nepal our permanent home.

To translate into words the wondrous experience of being in proximity to Dudjom Rinpoche is beyond my capacity. I prostrate to the source of all refuge, kindest lama, most exalted Lord of Wisdom.

KYABJE DUDJOM RINPOCHE

Wisdom Advice from the Lord of Refuge

ALL IS PERFECT FROM THE BEGINNING, essence of diamond, free of obscuration. To realize this, practice meditating beyond word or concept. View all appearances as illusion. Let them arise freely, without obstruction.

The difference between the sutras and the tantras is like the difference between the sky and the earth. According to the Tantrayana, we should not consider people to be friends or enemies but, instead, consider them to be naturally divine and an expression of wisdom. We also should consider our own body to be the nature of wisdom. What we must realize is "perfection from the beginning."

Intrinsically, we all have buddha nature—dharmakaya essence—complete, fully endowed and accomplished. Just as when one has jaundice, and the world appears washed in yellow, in this same way our own perceptions are now deluded.

When we do not recognize appearance as the pure display of self-arising dharmakaya awareness, grasping comes about. Perception and form manifest, and we cling to them; we also cling to the self who is grasping. Dualistic clinging takes us from our true nature, and we are left wandering in relative reality, exposed in the external world. Like it or not, we are temporarily trapped in samsaric existence. We must accept this and work toward enlightenment within the relative world. Until we realize that self and other are by nature without true existence, we rely on the Buddha, dharma and sangha. These sublime Three Jewels have the exalted means to draw us out of samsara.

Through the Buddha's compassion and the presence of the lama, we have the good fortune to receive the dharma teachings in our lives today. Outwardly, the lama is a link between the Buddha and ourselves. On a more extraordinary level, the lama is the manifestation of the Buddha's enlightened activity. That is why on the Vajrayana path, the lama is considered even more important than the Buddha.

We show respect for the lama not because he wants to be elevated or seeks our deference. We do so because of the sacredness, the profundity of the teachings and of the Buddhadharma itself.

No matter how exquisite your intellectual qualities and understanding, without devotion and respect, no spiritual teaching can take effect. Without devotion, even the compassion of all the buddhas cannot make it so. Those who have devotion harvest the blessings. Guru Rinpoche himself promised, "For whoever has devotion, I am there."

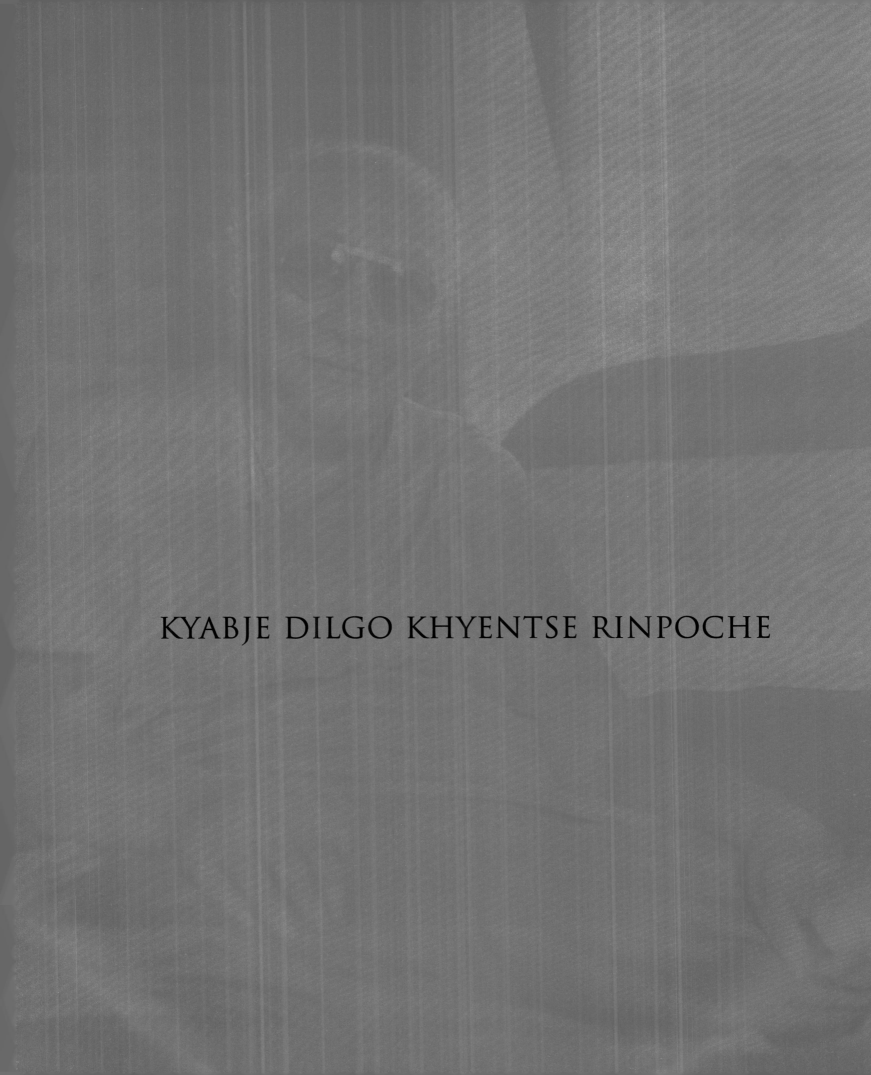

KYABJE DILGO KHYENTSE RINPOCHE

Meeting

KYABJE DILGO KHYENTSE RINPOCHE

THE MOMENT I SAW HIS HOLINESS DILGO KHYENTSE RINPOCHE, I was mesmerized by his hands, as many other students must have been. He had long, elegant fingers that moved expressively when he taught, a constant mudra of the divine. His voice was an unearthly rumble, his speech a continuously flowing river of the buddhas' sounds, his gaze all-seeing. For someone new to the dharma as I was, his extraordinary and holy appearance was indefinable, almost too much to absorb.

Students from all over the world journeyed to his monastery in Boudhanath to sit before this great guru and pray or receive his blessings. Masters from all four schools of Tibetan Buddhism and thousands of disciples came to him for teachings. Kyabje Dilgo Khyentse Rinpoche, whose ceaseless dharma activity filled the world with an ineffable radiance, was one of the most illustrious Dzogchen masters of the Nyingma lineage. In addition to discovering many termas, and giving countless teachings and initiations, during his lifetime Rinpoche wrote twenty-three volumes of scholarly texts and commentaries. Amazingly, he always seemed to have time for each one of his many devotees.

We stayed near his monastery in Nepal for many years and, in 1984, moved to the Dordogne region of France, where a small Buddhist community was developing near the famous prehistoric caves of Lascaux. His Holiness was teaching there at the time. The scenery in Dordogne is breathtaking in the spring, and when we arrived, the meadows were filled with yellow and fuchsia wildflowers swaying in the breeze under endless skies. Ancient castles were hidden from the road by tall birch trees, their silver trunks shimmering in early morning light. Dordogne seemed like the loveliest place on earth, with beauty greeting the eyes at every turn.

We settled in an old stone farmhouse on property being renovated for eventual use as a three-year retreat compound. Before we could unpack, the large snake that had taken up residence in the house had to be evicted. It zipped across the kitchen floor, into cabinets, over and under the beds. The previous tenants had lived quite happily with the snake, but my children wanted more privacy. It took four men nearly six hours to chase it out of the house.

Kyabje Dilgo Khyentse Rinpoche's home was not far, and every day a group of us would walk the short distance to La Sonnerie, where he was tirelessly conducting teachings and initiations. He would begin early in the morning and continue late into the evening, yet over several post-dawn sessions, he kindly made time to give a teaching for this book. On the last day, His Holiness placed his enormous hand over the top of my head, murmuring one of his constant blessings, and told me to return next year. His hallowed and miraculous voice never leaves my memory.

KYABJE DILGO KHYENTSE RINPOCHE

Freeing the Mind and Emotions

Your Holiness, emotions seem to be all-powerful and seduce us into believing they are real.
Will you please teach about this?

THE OBSCURING EMOTIONS OF ANGER, JEALOUSY, PRIDE, IGNORANCE AND DESIRE
are nothing but thoughts. But what are thoughts? When you watch a thought, look to see if it
has any substance or solidity. Does it have a color or shape? Can you find the place where the
thought has arisen? Can you find a place where it dwells? Can you find where it has gone when
it disappears from your mind?

When a negative thought like anger arises, look to see whether the thought itself and the ground from
which it arises are the same or different. Are they two different things? Generally speaking, when you
have many thoughts running through your mind, this is called "movement." It is the moving aspect
of the mind. Occasionally there are fewer thoughts, and the mind is quieter. This is called "quies-
cence," the still aspect of the mind. When you are conscious of having either many thoughts or few
thoughts, this is called "awareness." You should try to practice always being cognizant of whether
your thoughts are moving or still and so on. Try to observe your mind in this way. Then continuing
with the investigation, look to see whether the known and the knower—the object of this investigation and that which is investigating it—are two distinct things or the same. Meditate on the nature of
your mind. After a few days, come back and tell me what you find. By then you will have an answer.

Your Holiness, in the past few days, I've tried to meditate as you instructed,
but I must be doing something wrong. When I analyze the nature of my mind with my eyes closed,
it seems to manifest as shape and color. I find myself focusing on these colors and am beginning to
think the nature of my mind is the color blue! When my eyes are open, this division seems to dissolve.
[His Holiness laughs.]

You don't need to meditate with your eyes closed. If you look at the essence of mind with open eyes,
the aspects of clarity and intelligence come forth. You can close your eyes during shamatha (calm
abiding) when you want to stabilize or pacify your thoughts. But in the present case, as we are
watching the nature of mind, it is more like vipashyana (expansive vision or insight), in which you
should just see all appearances as they are. And as you said, you can then see things without too
much division or excessive distracted thought. Stay like this, seeing things but not entering into
them with many elaborate thoughts. Try to remain in that state.

Whenever a negative emotion like anger, desire or attachment appears, the first thing to do is to recognize that the thought is arising. Do not be blind to it. Once you have that recognition, you can watch it. Does it come from anywhere? Does it stay in any particular place? When it is no longer there, has it gone to any particular place? And as you investigate the thought, the only conclusion you can come to is that there is no such thing as this thought—that is, it has no form, no color and so forth. You can examine each and every thought in this way.

You may think that even though the thought has no substance, it still has a cause, something that is in some way permanent. For example, if the thought is one of hatred, you may think that it is caused by someone or something you don't like, something outside of yourself. This cannot be so, because the "enemy" is also simply a concept, a thought that if analyzed, just disintegrates. There is no entity that is intrinsically "your enemy." Moreover, how can something external be the true cause of your anger, which is inside you?

When you come to the conclusion that the thought is empty, remain in that emptiness. If, however, the emotion is strong and intractable and doesn't disappear, then look once again. Does it have any color or shape? Is there any place where it resides? In the end, there can be no option other than to return to emptiness. Remain in this emptiness. This is what you should do. Come back again after some time and tell me your experience. Then we will continue the teaching.

Due to impermanence and my lack of merit, I was unable to return
before His Holiness passed from this world.

MINDROLING TRICHEN RINPOCHE

Meeting

MINDROLING TRICHEN RINPOCHE

During our first years in Kathmandu, I heard many odd stories about an extraordinary mahasiddha in northern India who would rise from mystical sleep to greet devoted visitors with unexpected slaps on the back, taps on the head or other unusual modes of blessing. He was and still is revered throughout the Tibetan Buddhist community as one of the greatest living masters of our time, and I was very anxious to meet him. Some said that spending even a moment with His Holiness Mindroling Trichen Rinpoche was like being in a buddha land. In 1979 we set out for his monastery in Clementown, near the northern Indian hill station of Dehradun.

I love every aspect of India, including the chaos of road travel through her vast but crowded landscape. Motor scooters, bicycles and cars compete with ubiquitous trucks for space on the road, all of the drivers honking their horns madly. The trucks are each a work of art, no two ever the same. Their wooden sides are adorned with Coca-Cola advertisements and religious murals depicting Krishna, his indigo form dancing amid hot-pink lotus flowers, or Ganesh, the plump elephant god of good fortune. The windshields are strung with flashing Christmas lights; "Tata, Bye-bye" is cheekily stenciled on the rear bumper of every truck.

On this trip, we departed Delhi by bus, which naturally was filled to capacity with people and luggage. Wedged into cracked plastic seats at the far back, we had a chicken and two bleating goats as company for part of the ride as well. Upon arrival in Clementown, we went to Mindroling Rinpoche's home above the monastery to make offerings and at last meet this great saint. This first encounter was particularly memorable for my five-year-old son, Noah. When Rinpoche saw Noah, he smiled and beckoned him closer. He then reached for his own slipper and lightly and repeatedly struck my startled son on the back. The Tibetans in the room smiled, since being hit on the back by a great siddha is considered to be quite auspicious. And eventually, after ice cream and cookies, Noah also began to accept his good fortune.

Twenty years later, I returned to Clementown to request the teaching for this book. The train to Dehradun was scheduled to leave Delhi at 5:00 AM when the streets were still dark and the thieves still roaming. I was slightly concerned about going to the train station alone, but the frenetic pace in the station swept me along, leaving no time for unease. After the initial bedlam, taking the train in India is incredible fun. Visiting this exotic land is like looking into a kaleidoscope of pulsating color and action, but traveling on the railway system is like being catapulted straight into the display. Steam rises from the low train tracks, and the stations teem with people at all hours of the night and day. Agile coolies swarm you upon arrival, grab your ticket and head off for your train at a fast trot, luggage piled on their heads and backs, leaving you to rush after them. The exhaust belching from the old trains mingles with the smell of samosas and idli being fried on makeshift stoves and served on banana leaves. Families huddle together in the predawn darkness, the women dressed in bright saris, children grasping their silver tiffin boxes, and fathers with fat rolls of bedding under their arms in preparation for the long journey. Tea wallas jog from one train compartment to the next yelling, "Chai! Garam, garam chai!" and serving spicy sweet tea in disposable pottery cups. Bleary-eyed travelers crowd the train doors, bargaining for snacks, newspapers, Orange Squash.

The inside of the train compartment turns into a traveling picnic where friends are immediately made over the bridge of shared food. Glass bangles tinkle as women oil and braid their daughters' long black hair. Hours pass slowly. The swaying of the train clacking along the tracks brings a drowsy lull to the conversations, and frequent stops are made in the middle of India's flatlands for no apparent reason. Still, my destination of Dehradun seemed to arrive too soon.

The city of Dehradun had changed since my last visit from a moderately dusty, inconvenient hill station to a bustling and traffic-logged, inconvenient city. The Egg & Toast Guest House where we had stayed so many years ago was no longer in business, so the taxi driver recommended another hotel. Our destination seemed dubious as he drove me down an alley lined with refuse, but the Regent Hotel turned out to be an old mansion built during the British occupation and now converted to a lovely, slightly surreal guest house. The entryway opened to a huge ballroom with crystal chandeliers and a marble floor, its expansive interior empty except for a couch and small registration desk perched on a platform in one corner. My call of "Hello?" echoed in the converted ballroom, and a heavily accented voice called back, "Yes, yes, please come in, Madam. Grandmother is just now making lunch, so please tell her what you would like to eat." I spent the day resting in that abandoned palace, surrounded by the faded elegance of the British Raj.

Early the next morning, I hired a taxi and set out for Mindroling Trichen Rinpoche's monastery. Within a few minutes, the traffic of Dehradun was left behind, and the road narrowed to little more than a rock and dirt path. The taxi soon came upon a plodding cart pulled by two water buffaloes and loaded with bamboo. The poles stretched across the entire breadth of the road, rocking back and forth as the buffaloes stumbled over potholes. No one could pass, and the insouciant bullock driver didn't even glance back to acknowledge the incessant honking by the many thwarted drivers. A procession of vehicles soon developed behind the cart, and I enjoyed a very unhurried ride to the monastery.

It was stunning to see Mindroling Monastery and the community that had developed around it. In addition to the main compound, there are primary and secondary schools, retreat centers, libraries, and a college offering the most advanced levels of scholarly training. Mindroling Monastery is one of the largest Nyingma centers of Buddhist learning in India today. On the grounds stands a majestic stupa symbolizing Buddha Shakyamuni's descent from Devaloka. Walking closer, I saw that the stupa was still under construction. Within its dome-shaped base were hundreds of golden buddhas. Two monks moved reverently among the statues, painting the faces with delicate, precise strokes. The top of the stupa resembled a vase, embedded with golden steps. A lifelike form of Buddha Shakyamuni stood poised in midstep on the staircase, and above him sat the figure of the future Buddha Maitreya, his eyes gazing into space with promise. How comforting it was to be assured of the buddhas' continuing manifestations.

When I saw Mindroling Rinpoche, I prostrated before him. Rinpoche beckoned me to come closer; then smiling, he grabbed a fistful of my hair and tugged it playfully and repeatedly. This blessing will stay with me until I return. The next morning, Rinpoche offered the following words for the readers of this book.

MINDROLING TRICHEN RINPOCHE

Truth and Courage

THE ESSENCE OF DHARMA lies in being true to oneself (one's innate nature) and in exerting great effort to be courageous. When truth and the courage to walk on the path of truth are joined with mindfulness, a practitioner truly begins to practice the dharma. Until these qualities of truth and courage are generated, we will be vulnerable to our own pretenses and fabrications.

The arising of truth and courage allows us to realize the core essence of dharma. Not understanding this leads us into the trap of endless cyclic existence. A lack of courage keeps us from being true to our buddha nature.

Both virtuous and nonvirtuous actions are formed in the mind. Actions—though more apparent—are secondary to our motivation. Even an apparently virtuous action is of little benefit if the root of our motivation is selfishness. Any action performed with wisdom and selfless motivation is an expression of our own buddha nature.

PENOR RINPOCHE

Meeting

PENOR RINPOCHE

PENOR RINPOCHE'S SEAT IN INDIA, NAMDROLING MONASTERY, is home to more than three thousand monks, nuns and lamas, most all of whom are provided for solely by Penor Rinpoche. It was not always so, and the story of Namdroling's origins that was told to me by one of Rinpoche's close students is so inspiring that it should be recounted here. After Rinpoche was forced to leave Tibet, he made his way to the south of India with only 300 rupees and a few monks to help him rebuild his monastery. Rinpoche himself began the construction, enduring immense hardship in the process. In the sweltering heat of South India, he carried stones, bricks and sand, and mixed cement until his hands and feet bled. Still he continued. The lack of water and roads made the work even more difficult. People would ask him why he needed a monastery as large as the one he had planned when there were so few monks. They urged him to build something smaller, but Rinpoche persisted. Today, attendance at Namdroling Monastery is so high that the grand assembly hall often fills to overflowing.

Given the importance of education in the Buddhist tradition, I was eager to visit this large and vital Nyingma center of learning and practice. But before I could make the journey, Rinpoche came to the Bay Area to teach. I met with him, not at his monastery, but in a quintessential California abode with a sea of pristine white carpeting, bright with flowers and soft sunlight. His presence was serious and majestic but also very soothing. I experienced a strange dichotomy— awed to be sitting before such an exalted being and yet oddly relaxed, as if he had instilled in me a sense of calm and confidence.

Penor Rinpoche spoke about the guru–disciple relationship. It might be tempting to think that our own questions about guru devotion are unique to our culture. But when Rinpoche taught, we could have been anywhere—in the high plains of Tibet a thousand years ago, the South Indian desert, or the California bungalow we were sitting in that day—and his words, so pointed and orderly, would have had the same powerful resonance. Penor Rinpoche's teachings give us a kind yet authoritative reminder: cultural biases do not in any way mitigate the sanctity and importance of the guru–disciple relationship.

PENOR RINPOCHE

Guru Devotion

GENERALLY SPEAKING, WHEN WE FOLLOW A SPIRITUAL PATH such as the path of Buddhism, it is essential to find a qualified teacher or master and rely upon that teacher's guidance. Anyone who attains enlightenment does so by relying upon teachers as part of the process. Students receive profound instructions from a master, put them into practice and thus gain the result. This doesn't come about automatically. This doesn't come about haphazardly. Nor is it something that people can decipher on their own. However, in relying upon a master, you shouldn't be naive, taking any teacher who comes along and accepting without question whatever is said. You must be discriminating: examine whether, at the very least, the teacher has compassion for the students.

Above and beyond that, you must verify the lineage. What is the origin of the teachings you are receiving? This is very important. The teacher must be someone who is passing on a valid tradition, someone who holds and transmits an authentic lineage. This lineage must have been maintained by great spiritual beings generation after generation without any interruption due to broken commitments, impaired samaya or some other disruptive factor. Such a lineage can be compared to a beautiful golden thread that has not been tarnished in any way and remains bright, immaculate and well-polished over succeeding generations. Reliance upon a compassionate teacher who holds this kind of lineage will truly benefit you as a practitioner.

There is a special relationship that develops between a spiritual master and a student. From the master's perspective, facilitating the student's spiritual development is the primary responsibility. The master must clearly discern the student's strengths and weaknesses to determine whether the student will be a suitable recipient of a specific teaching. The teacher must assess how stable the student's mind is and how sharp his intellect. But it is not necessarily a question of the student's intelligence; faith and trust are also considerations. How much does the student trust the teacher? The teacher has to gauge this in order to work effectively with the student.

From the student's perspective, what is most important is a sense of trust that expresses itself as faith and devotion. Ideally, you respond to your teacher as you would if the Buddha had walked into the room and you were relating directly to him. You may feel this faith as a sense of awe, a sense of yearning, a sense of confidence in the teacher's instructions and what he embodies. This is essential for the relationship to be a truly successful one, a truly effective one. The student's faith must become unshakable so that there is complete trust in the teacher's guidance.

You can listen carefully to the teacher's advice and integrate it into your own spiritual practice. Under certain circumstances, the teacher may say things that you find inappropriate or startling, or may act in ways that seem wrathful or completely out of context. Should this happen, remember what the primary nature of the relationship is. It is not for you as the student to become entangled in value judgments about what the master is or is not doing. Rather, listen to what the teacher is saying to you on the level of your own practice, and make certain you are carrying it out. This is the most essential thing for you as a student to focus on.

There is a deep bond of love and affection between a teacher and student. The teacher relates to the student as a mother would to her only child. In Buddhism we aspire to feel such loving kindness toward all beings, whether we are teachers or students.

What if we feel that our devotion is inadequate? How do we increase our devotion?

That is really your own responsibility because no one can do it for you. You have to find ways to inspire yourself, whether we're talking about devotion and faith, bodhicitta, altruism or compassion. There are a few individuals for whom inspiration is quite natural. They are just born that way, so to speak. But most of us have to work at it. We have to identify the qualities we need, notice where they're lacking and seek ways to encourage them in ourselves.

When we want something very much, such as a lover, there is no lack of inspiration;
it almost seems similar to devotion. When we yearn for ice cream, we have no difficulty
listening carefully to directions and going one-pointedly to the nearest ice cream shop.
How does this kind of surrendering to a desired object differ from devotion?

What you say is true. We must distinguish between our ordinary attachment to people, things or situations and the purer quality of devotion we feel toward the teacher. The ordinary way in which we are attached to something, however much it may seem to inspire us, is rooted in the afflictive emotion of desire; there is something we want to possess. In comparison, the devotion we feel for a master is based upon a sense of humility, a sense of respect for what we are receiving from the teacher, so there is quite a different tone to the situation.

Critical thinking is part of our training in the Western educational system.
Trust is seldom emphasized. Also, our society has a strong belief in the need
for personal freedom, and some view religion as restrictive.

There is plenty of personal freedom in Buddhism. Buddhism is not a set of rules someone laid down for us to follow and does not really operate on the principle of "Thou shalt not." Nor does it emphasize, "You can do this but you cannot do that," "You mustn't think this or you mustn't say that." In a sense, we could think of Buddhism as being completely open. All the Buddha said was that if you act in a certain way, it will lead you to greater states of happiness and ultimately enlightenment, and if you act in another way, it will bring about increased suffering and lower states of rebirth. The choice is yours. Buddhism is based upon clearly delineating choices and understanding their consequences. People are free to decide as they wish.

That said, the only fruitful approach on the Buddhist path is to have confidence in the enlightened qualities of the Buddha and the efficacy of his teachings. To examine the teachings is fine. To contemplate them, turn them over in your mind, reflect upon their meaning and apply them to your experience—all that is fine. However, to be critical or cynical about the teachings or the teacher is counterproductive. Many people are engaged in examining the Buddhist teachings, but to do so properly requires a sense of respect for the teachings.

Furthermore, let's be clear on the vastness of our inquiry. We should understand that examining the incredible qualities of buddhahood will be quite challenging. Our ordinary minds don't even know what will happen to us tomorrow, let alone comprehend the unfathomable qualities of the Buddha.

Buddhahood is a state of omniscience, which includes the ability to be aware of the constitutions and situations of each and every being. Whatever a given being is thinking from moment to moment, whatever words that being is speaking from moment to moment, every aspect of that being's experience, activity or behavior is completely open to the wisdom and knowing quality of an enlightened mind. This omniscience is not subject to the personal biases and emotional reactions that characterize our ordinary knowing. When a buddha teaches, the power of his speech is such that all beings present hear the teachings directly in their own language and in a manner they can understand.

Once while traveling in India, the Buddha encountered three people. One was a sick man, one the physician taking care of him and the other a nurse. The Buddha spoke only one phrase, but each of the three heard something different. The patient heard, "Trust your physician and take the medicine he prescribes." The physician heard, "Have real concern for your patient and be very intent on curing him." And the nurse heard, "Take good care of your patient, help the doctor treat him and the patient will be cured." All three heard the words appropriate to their own situation.

Another story tells of a great siddha, an accomplished master, who set out with a large group of people on an arduous journey over a mountain pass. It was a hot day, and when they reached the pass, the weary travelers sat down to rest. One of them mentioned that some yogurt would be delightfully cooling and refreshing, but no one had any. The siddha took from his robes a skullcup that he used as an eating bowl. He held it up behind himself, and somehow the bowl started filling up with sweet yogurt as if from the sky. This continued until everyone had been refreshed.

The point of the story is this: when you master the unity of emptiness and compassion in your own mind, it endows you with command of your environment and an ability to affect the experience of others in a way that benefits them very directly. When I speak about the Buddhadharma as an extraordinary path, deeply profound, exalted above all others, it is because I understand that the qualities the teachings refer to are there for anyone to attain. Those who put these teachings into practice will find benefit, not only in this life but also in future lives. They will ultimately awaken to the supremely blissful state of enlightenment. That is why it is so important that we comprehend the principles of the dharma and apply them appropriately in our own lives. Then we obtain the results of our practice. We gain the attainment we seek.

So my final words to you are: Please, when you embrace these teachings, embrace them wholeheartedly. Practice the dharma very carefully and methodically. Practice with all of your heart.

DODRUPCHEN RINPOCHE

Meeting
DODRUPCHEN RINPOCHE

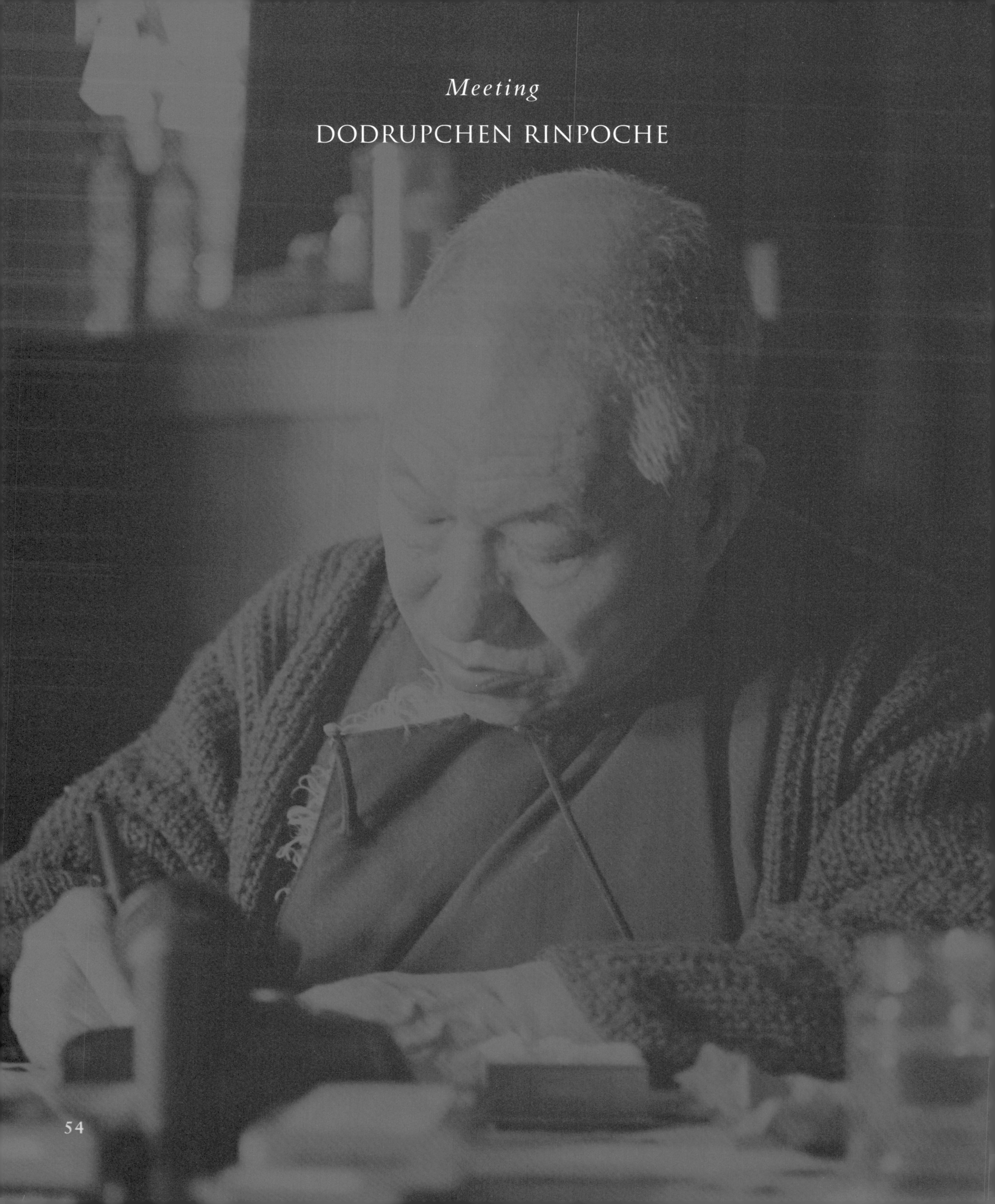

DODRUPCHEN RINPOCHE IS ONE OF THE GREAT HEADS OF THE NYINGMA SCHOOL and a holder of the Longchen Nyingtik lineage. We first met this supreme master in 1980 during a series of initiations in Clementown. The children had come with me, and my daughter's health had not fared well during the long journey from Nepal to India. The mother of the Tibetan family we were staying with told me that everyone in the community had absolute trust in Dodrupchen Rinpoche's divinations, and we should seek his advice. So the following morning I took my daughter to see Rinpoche, hoping that he could help her more than the doctor had been able to. Rinpoche looked at the two of us with great concern and told us to return the next day for a long-life initiation and blessing. Although we were strangers, he showed immense softness and caring. I felt immediate trust and relief as well as gratitude for such wholehearted attention to a child's needs and a mother's worry. As it happened, my daughter recovered within days of having received Rinpoche's blessings.

In 2001 my friend Penzom Lama and I traveled to Rinpoche's monastery, Chorten Gompa, in Gangtok, Sikkim, to request that Rinpoche give a teaching for this book. A taxi dropped us off at the bottom of a hill, and we walked the rest of the way up roughly paved paths and stone steps. It was an exceptionally clear day, and the unobstructed mountain air coated our lungs like cold silk. The immense white dome of the stupa built near Rinpoche's monastery seemed to rise out of the hill as we ascended, growing bigger with every step. Perhaps it was the unique light in Gangtok or the reflection from the snow mountains above, but a brilliant white light radiated from the dome. As we came closer, the deep blue statue of Vajrakilaya standing high atop the stupa revealed his magnificent wrathful face.

We had arrived quite early and joined the group of devotees holding plates mounded with eggs, fruit and roasted barley flour as offerings for Rinpoche. No one had come empty-handed. When the attendant opened the door, women with children tied to their backs, yogins, and distant visitors like us all silently streamed into the monastery. In spite of the large number of people, there was an air of simplicity and peaceful discipline, all those present conducting themselves with grace and respect. It was as if just being in proximity to Rinpoche imbued everyone with greater mindfulness and refinement.

As we entered, Khandro Pema Dechen greeted us with an ageless energy and enthusiasm. She and Penzom were particularly happy to see one another and chatted for some time. Khandro eventually sent us to Rinpoche's room, where we watched as visitors came with their offerings and questions. Rinpoche gave each one his full attention just as he had done for us in Clementown years before. One request was especially poignant: a European woman asked for a prediction regarding her seven-year-old son, who was extremely ill, in the hope that prayers or pujas could be done to cure him. It may well have been my imagination, but as Rinpoche completed the divination, it seemed that a flash of deep sorrow crossed his face. Penzom later told me the prediction had indicated that the boy might not fully recover in this life; Rinpoche hadn't wanted to tell the mother because he knew the pain such news would cause. In my mind, the empathy and compassion reflected in his face offered a true glimpse of the Buddha's love.

When it came our turn to speak with Rinpoche, we prostrated three times, made our offerings and showed him the letter from Dudjom Rinpoche that encouraged the production of this book. We requested teachings on compassion, and in response Rinpoche spoke the words that follow.

On the way out, we saw that the line of visitors had grown even longer, and the attendant told us that each morning is the same. Rinpoche sees a great many people who ask for blessings and counsel. Dodrupchen Rinpoche's vast kindness is a sheltering blanket for his students and the community at large. His presence is a sanctuary.

DODRUPCHEN RINPOCHE

Compassion Meditation

Rinpoche, would you please give us some guidance on helping those who are suffering?
Sometimes we're at a loss as to what to do when others are in pain, so we simply ignore them.
At other times, we feel that their own actions have caused their distress, so we blame them and excuse
ourselves from helping. How can we avoid such judgements and give true assistance to others?

YOU CAN DO THIS MEDITATION ON BODHICITTA ANYWHERE, ANYTIME, and it will be beneficial: When you see a person suffering, you should think of all the countless others who are hurting in exactly the same way. Although it is true our pain is a consequence of our karma and does not come about without cause and condition, still we must encourage thoughts of compassion within ourselves. So wherever and whenever you see someone in distress, remind yourself of the pervasive nature of suffering and hold these thoughts:

> May I take on this suffering for other beings.
> May this suffering ripen within me instead of them.
> May not even a single sentient being experience this kind of suffering.
> May it be so.

Then continue and expand your compassion meditation, sincerely wishing:

> May all sentient beings be parted from their suffering.
> How fervently I wish this to be so.
> May they never experience suffering.
> How wonderful it would be if others no longer endured any torment.
> I will work hard to eradicate all the suffering of beings.

There are many attitudes we can have toward suffering, but this outlook of compassion is what we should meditate upon.

Rinpoche, it seems as though we often become absorbed in our own good circumstances
and forget about the purpose of the bodhisattva path.
How can we use our fortunate conditions to increase compassion and love?

When you experience personal joy and happiness, you should recognize this as the compassionate blessing of the Three Jewels and all the buddhas and bodhisattvas. Stop and think,

"What is this good fortune?" and answer, "This is the blessing of the Three Jewels." Do this even in everyday situations, such as when you feel very hot in the sun and a moment of cool breeze gives you relief. Recognize even this cooling air as the kindness and good wishes of the buddhas and bodhisattvas, who constantly embrace sentient beings of the six realms. With each moment of happiness think, "Here I am, experiencing their blessing." In this way, you can use your good circumstances as an opportunity to develop faith and pure vision toward the Three Jewels, the buddhas and the bodhisattvas. Then your compassion will increase.

You have to train yourself in this manner because your mind will develop in whatever way you direct it. Since all occurrences and all phenomena are dependent on mind, your personal experience will be a reflection of how you have trained your own mind.

For those of us who are followers of the Buddhist path, we need to do as Lord Buddha taught. Among his teachings are guidelines for how we should and should not conduct ourselves. I know it is very hard to follow his words exactly, but still you need to do your best. You should think thus: "I know it is difficult, but I *can* train my mind and *will* follow the Buddha's way."

Thank you, Rinpoche. In some cultures,
we are encouraged to think first of ourselves and our own needs.

Yes, and clinging to the self, we think, "May *my* life be happier, may *my* life be better, may *I* be perfectly content." This is what we call desire or attachment—the desire for personal happiness and love. This selfishness or self-cherishing is the main cause of suffering and rebirth within the circle of life. This selfish thought is the very root of sorrow.

How can we counteract this, Rinpoche?

By the practice of bodhicitta. We speak of sentient beings as "borderless," meaning that living beings pervade all of space. There are birds whose home is the sky, fish who inhabit the water, others who walk the earth and so on. And among all these beings, there is not a single one who at some time or another has not been your father or mother. And when they were your parent, they cherished and loved you in the same way your present mother does or in the same way you adore your own child.

A person familiar with Buddhism will understand this idea. To others it may sound like a story or a fairy tale. This is why you have to read and study Buddha's teachings. Although it may be hard to comprehend, there is not a single being you have not already loved and who has not loved you in the past.

Remembering this, you should think, "Now I am going to practice the dharma in order to completely destroy the suffering of all beings. What should I do to accomplish this? How can I help these many beloved beings?" First, you should decide you will do no harm to others. And then think, "Whatever is in my capacity to give, that I will give, and I will do it well. Ultimately, through the practice of bodhicitta, I will work wholeheartedly to liberate all beings from this world of sorrow, leaving not even a single one behind."

We should train our minds with these thoughts. There is no more concise and essential teaching than what is contained here in this short practice of compassion. As Buddhists, we should meditate on this until we understand the true meaning of bodhicitta, the mind of awakening.

May it be so.

CHADRAL SANGYE DORJE RINPOCHE

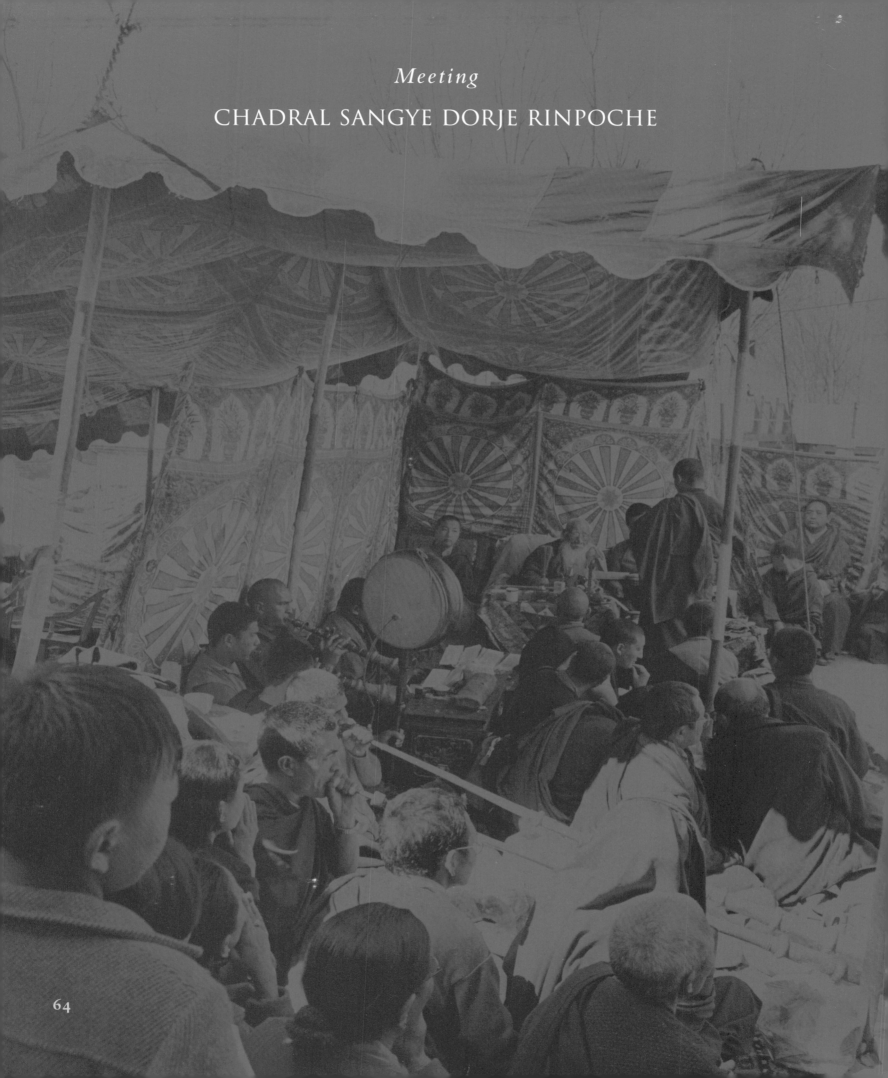

CHADRAL SANGYE DORJE RINPOCHE WAS THE FIRST BUDDHIST MASTER we met upon arriving in Kathmandu in 1977. Although I had come to study with Kyabje Dudjom Rinpoche, when I reached his house with my two young children in tow, we found that he was out of the country. We stood somewhat forlornly outside Dudjom Rinpoche's gate while sheets of monsoon rain churned the driveway into a brown river of mud. I spoke no Nepali, but a kind member of his household gestured to me and guided us down an alley lined with carpet shops smelling of damp wool. Not knowing where we were being led or why, we followed the splash of his plastic thongs through the lanes of Kathmandu. I clasped the children's hands tightly, dodging rickshaws and jumping puddles. Our guide led us through a low doorway and up a dark and narrow staircase. There at the top, in a small room dusky with incense, sat Chadral Rinpoche. Light filtered through the gracefully carved shutter of a small window, falling gently on Rinpoche's face. Just seeing him, I felt all my fears lift and sensed we were in the company of a great master.

Every inch of the floor, the cushions and the bed was covered with Tibetan carpets, the riot of patterns and shades creating a brightly colored cocoon. We sat quietly with Rinpoche, the children tracing the unfamiliar patterns of wool dragons and snow lions, eating Indian sugar biscuits, and tasting salty yak butter tea for the first time. Chadral Rinpoche placed silky red blessing cords around our necks; then in a deep but gentle voice, he reassured me that Dudjom Rinpoche would be returning soon. I was grateful for such a kind and fortuitous welcome, and we walked back into the summer rain feeling comforted and happy. From that day on, we visited Chadral Rinpoche often to ask his wisdom advice and receive his blessings.

Over time, I began to think of Chadral Rinpoche as the great-grandfather and protector of the Nyingma tradition. He is revered as a true saint and one of the oldest Dzogchen masters alive today. The name "Chadral"—meaning "one who has abandoned mundane activities"—was given him during his nomadic years in Tibet. Having left his family home at the age of fifteen, he dedicated his life to dharma practice. For many years, he traveled across the mountains and plains of Tibet on foot, studying with the great masters and staying in remote caves for long periods of solitary retreat. Now Rinpoche resides primarily in Pharping, Nepal, a place of extraordinary natural beauty made more so by the fact that it is one of the major pilgrimage sites for devotees of Padmasambhava. And while Chadral Rinpoche preserves the tradition of his name, maintaining a very quiet existence, people still come from all over the world hoping to meet him. In his later years, Rinpoche has built retreat centers and monasteries as well as many exquisite temples and stupas in Nepal and India.

It was important to me that Rinpoche's teachings and images be included in this book. However, since his words do not often appear in English publications, I requested a teaching with some trepidation. At my first appeal, Rinpoche said, "Hmmm," and immediately turned his attention to another visitor. When he looked my way again, I added that although many in the West know we must avoid taking life, most of us are unfamiliar with the spiritual practice of saving lives, that is, buying animals destined for slaughter and setting them free. I asked Rinpoche if he would please give us a teaching on this topic. Again he said, "Hmmm," and fell silent. I eventually took leave without an answer. Later his daughter Saraswati told me that Rinpoche had agreed to give a teaching on ransoming and saving lives.

Every year, Rinpoche himself journeys to Calcutta to buy thousands of live fish that are slated to be killed and releases them into the Indian Ocean. Hundreds of people contribute to a fund established specifically for this purpose, and all royalties from *Sacred Voices* will be dedicated to saving the lives of such helpless beings. In this way, the readers of this book will be following Chadral Rinpoche's esteemed example. May this soothe those beings who are frightened and alone.

CHADRAL SANGYE DORJE RINPOCHE

The Ransom and Release of Animals

To the spiritual master, Buddha of Infinite Life, Amitayus,
And to his bodhisattva disciples, I bow.
I will now briefly explain the benefits
Of ransoming and releasing animals.

To ransom and release animals
Constitutes a flawless practice
To be done with pure motivation and applied
By all of Shakyamuni's followers.

The benefits of this practice have been described extensively
In many sutras, tantras and treatises.
Oceanlike gatherings of learned and accomplished masters of India and Tibet
Have considered this an important way to aid beings.

For those of the Hinayana,
This practice represents the abandoning of harming others;
For those who have entered the mind of awakening of the Mahayana,
It represents the training itself;
And for practitioners of the Secret Mantra,
It represents the principal tantric commitment of the Jewel buddha family.

The reason for this is that in the world,
Nothing is more precious than life itself
And no negative act more serious than taking life.
Therefore, among composite forms of the roots of virtue,
None has greater benefit
Than the ransom and release of animals.
If you wish for happiness and good fortune,
Be diligent on this supreme path.

The authenticity of this practice is proven
By the authority of scripture and by logic.
It is a path without obstacle or error.
Thinking of your own body as an example,
Through this practice, give up harming others.

Don't take life.
Instead, release birds, fish, wild animals,
Farm animals doomed to be slaughtered
And also small creatures such as ants and bees.
Be diligent in giving them refuge from fear.

The benefits of this are inconceivable:
It is the supreme practice for longevity,
And there is no higher practice for nurturing good health
Or for dedicating virtue to the dead.
It is my main practice to help beings.

It clears away misfortune that arises due to outer and inner obstacles
And creates harmonious circumstances effortlessly and spontaneously.
When it is guided by positive motivation
And concluded with pure dedication and aspirations,
Its effect is that you will reach perfect enlightenment
And accomplish the two goals—benefit for yourself and for others.
Have no doubt of this!

Those who are endowed with merit and a virtuous attitude
Should prevent the practice of hunting in mountains and valleys.
In particular, during autumn and spring,
When flocks of cranes and other birds
Are compelled by their karma to fly south or north,
They must move their wings with great effort
And soar through space.
Yet sometimes they must come to earth
With anxiety, fear and an uneasy mind.

Don't hit such beings with stones or weapons.
Don't kill or harm them.
Protect them and help them continue their migration in comfort.

"To help with loving-kindness
Destitute beings without protection
Has merit equal to that of
Meditating on the essence of compassion and emptiness."
Thus said the glorious master Atisha.

Lamas, masters, monks, nuns and lay people, both women and men,
Should each in your own domain
Energetically perform as much ransom and release of animals as you are able.
And encourage others to do the same.

By doing so,
You will pacify sickness and disaster
Among humans and farm animals in your region.
Harvests will be plentiful, crops will increase, life will be long
And perfect happiness will dawn.
The time of death will be free of pain and confusion.
In the next life, you will attain an excellent body in a pleasant realm,
And eventually you will easily attain the supreme state of perfect awakening.
Have no doubt of this!

I, the one known as Chadral Sangye Dorje,
Am always devoted to the activity of ransoming and releasing life.

By the virtue of these words,
May all beings enter the way of the bodhisattvas.

Mama Koling Samanta.

TRULSHIK RINPOCHE

Meeting

TRULSHIK RINPOCHE

AMONG THE NYINGMAPAS, it is not uncommon for both teachers and students to maintain the life of a householder while wholeheartedly following the spiritual path. In contrast, the eminent Trulshik Rinpoche is a holder of the Vinaya, the monastic tradition. The vows of a monk or nun can be received only from one who is fully ordained, so Nyingma practitioners wishing to take such vows often request them from the revered Trulshik Rinpoche.

Rinpoche lives in Solo Khumbu, Nepal, where he went into exile after the Communist occupation of Tibet. He has stayed for forty years in this remote region near Mount Everest, spending much of his time in solitary retreat. He has also built a monastery there, Thubden Choling, which today houses more than five hundred nuns and two hundred monks, with many more waiting to become residents. There is no access to the monastery by road, so going there involves a ten-day trek from Kathmandu. The trail traces the route to Everest base camp and is said to be stunningly beautiful, but the climb, reaching an altitude of ten thousand feet, is very rigorous. In spite of my eagerness to go, I was concerned about having adequate strength to complete the trek. However, many of the masters I had spoken to about this book emphasized Rinpoche's importance to the Nyingma lineage and urged me to receive teachings from him. So in the year 2000, I again traveled to Kathmandu, planning to visit his monastery.

When I arrived at the airport, a friend told me that Rinpoche was actually in Boudhanath, right outside the city, but that he might be leaving very soon. We quickly loaded the suitcases into the car and went in search of Rinpoche. He was completing a series of initiations in a small monastery near Boudha stupa. Devotees overflowed from the shrine room, filling the surrounding brick patio. Trulshik Rinpoche sat serenely on a throne, surrounded by many monks, nuns and lay practitioners. He was chanting in low tones that resounded in the crowded courtyard, and his face was as radiant as the full moon. We waited until the initiations were finished, then went to receive Rinpoche's blessings and request that he teach for this book. He graciously agreed to do so, but informed me that he was leaving early the next morning for Dordogne, France. He said he could give a teaching there.

In the autumn of that year, I followed Rinpoche to France. Dordogne is home to several drupdras (literally, places of accomplishment) where diligent dharma students undertake spiritual practice in seclusion for three years, three months and three days. Rinpoche was instructing these retreatants when I arrived, but he emerged from the drupdra to give a teaching for the book. Tulku Pema Rinpoche escorted this treasured master and translated his words. Trulshik Rinpoche spoke for more than an hour, his voice smooth and continuous, his presence the essence of wisdom.

TRULSHIK RINPOCHE

Taming Our Mind

Our Lord Buddha told us:

> "Abandon evildoing.
> Practice virtue well.
> Master your own mind."
> This is the Buddha's teaching.

When we say, "Abandon evildoing," we refer both to negative actions that we may consciously commit with our body, speech or mind, as well as to our more subtle, unconscious habitual propensities and turbulent emotions. The Buddha identified 84,000 mental defilements. As antidotes to these, he gave 84,000 different teachings on taming the mind.

The problem underlying all of these defilements is the division we make between self and others. Attachment, aversion and ignorance spring from this division. As we all know, we have keen attachment to our dear ones and strong aversion to those we think are against us. Also, we feel indifferent toward those more distant from us, which is a subtle form of aversion.

Within the mind, attachment and aversion have a high profile and are easy to recognize. In contrast, ignorance stays quite hidden and is not easy to discern. But whether attachment, aversion and ignorance are conspicuous or subtle, we must release ourselves from their grip. In undertaking this task, the most important step is to become more aware of what is happening within the mind so that it can be tamed. That is why the Buddha gave teachings on the four types of mindfulness. The first is mindfulness of actions; the second, mindfulness of sensations and feelings; the third, mindfulness of the nature of phenomena; and the fourth, mindfulness of mind. I will speak briefly today about these four kinds of mindfulness.

To develop mindfulness of actions, we must become aware of our behavior as well as its consequences. There are many kinds of negative actions, but in essence we can group them into ten categories: three of body, four of speech and three of mind.

The first negative action of body is killing or putting the lives of others in danger. Take our treatment of animals as an example. We kill them mindlessly without respect for how the animals feel. The antidote to this negative action is to develop empathy. Think of how very important your own

life is to you. Is life not equally valuable to all beings? Surely it must be; and if that is so, we should not misuse our power as humans by endangering the lives of these poor creatures. The reason all killing is so horrific is that life is the single most precious thing for all of us, whether we are humans or animals. There is nothing we can do that is more harmful than taking a precious life.

The second negative action of the body is stealing. Stealing not only involves taking others' possessions by force. It also includes cheating and secretly taking advantage of others' belongings or misusing them without their knowledge.

The third negative action of body is sexual misconduct. This includes forcing people into sexual acts, committing rape, indulging in sex just for one's own satisfaction without regard for the other and using sex as a way to take advantage of a situation. These negative actions of killing, stealing and sexual misconduct all lead to a great deal of suffering.

The four negative actions of speech are telling lies, creating conflict through divisive speech, using harsh words and wasting valuable time in idle talk.

There are three negative actions of mind. The first is coveting, wanting to possess what others have—for example, harboring a secret desire to obtain their wealth. The second is bearing ill-will toward others. The third is holding wrong views—for example, due to our ignorance, not having confidence in the Three Jewels, not accepting that suffering is the result of negative action or thinking that happiness cannot be gained through positive action.

All of these negative actions will eventually result in suffering and are obstacles on the path to enlightenment. To avoid actions that will have unpleasant repercussions in our lives, to avoid pain, we must strive to gain control over our own minds. We should approach each day with mindfulness, carefully avoiding negative actions and trying our best to accumulate positive actions. Such mindfulness will lead to peace with others and within ourselves.

To further tame the mind, we must develop the second kind of mindfulness—mindfulness of sensations and feelings. For this, we should try to increase our awareness of the sensations that arise as we see, hear or taste something. This will protect us from becoming enslaved by attraction and aversion to the objects of our senses. For instance, alcoholism begins with the mere taste of an alcoholic drink; gradually, we are more and more caught by that taste and the accompanying sensation to the point that we become addicted.

We have to be continually aware of our feelings and sensations. For example, many of us are attached to the tastes we experience while eating meat. We should be aware of this as we eat, trying to go beyond the sensations. To do so, we begin by thinking about where the meat has come from. First of all, our consumption of meat is dependent on the death of another living creature. That animal does not die with joy and peace, but in pain and fear. Every fiber of meat is mixed with its agony. Eating meat may bring us temporary pleasure, but it will inevitably affect our physical or mental health and bring us suffering in this and future lifetimes.

Smoking also begins as a mere sensation, then spirals into addiction. Texts detailing the origins of its harmful effects explain that tobacco is not an ordinary plant. Long ago, a demon king called Karbunchok, together with his queen and ministers, supplicated negative forces with the malevolent wish that whoever smoked these leaves would bring immense trouble upon themselves, lose all the mental control necessary to maintain the right view and so be led to the lower realms. As you know, smoking is the cause of many diseases. No one is happy to be diagnosed with cancer, which can definitely be brought about by smoking. And you can calculate for yourself how much money one has to spend to maintain the habit.

This is all the more so for those who use drugs and thereby squander all of their wealth and possessions. Taking intoxicants is harmful because these addictive substances disturb our mental clarity. Alcohol has nothing but defects and can do no good for anyone. Those who become addicted often place their families in situations of conflict. All addictions impair our lives and health and in the end can only bring suffering. Being aware of these facts and trying to develop mindfulness of sensation will help us avoid addiction.

The third kind of mindfulness is mindfulness of the nature of phenomena. This consists of developing the capacity to understand and realize the ultimate nature of things. It starts from an awareness of the dynamic of cause and effect. This dynamic is particularly important for understanding what underlies all suffering. In general, there is not a single being who does not undergo the suffering of birth, aging, sickness and death. Regardless of whether you believe in karma and past lives, you cannot say, "There is no such thing as suffering. There is no such thing as sickness. There is no such thing as aging. There is no such thing as death." All beings have to go through these experiences, and how they do so depends upon their actions in past lives.

We cannot deny the suffering we encounter even during our daily activities. From the time we wake up in the morning until we go to bed at night, we experience all sorts of stress and sorrow, especially in these degenerate times. Being separated from those we love and having to be with people we don't like brings us suffering. Not getting what we want and getting what we don't want brings us suffering. There may be some people who do not undergo all these kinds of suffering every day, but they are quite rare.

As the Buddha said, to overcome this torment we first need to know its cause. I have already explained that the root of our suffering is negative actions and conflicting emotions, such as attachment, anger and ignorance. But just to recognize the cause is not enough. We need a method to overcome these conflicting emotions. Such a method is the meditation practice of shamatha, or sustained calm.

To develop this meditation, take advantage of the most favorable conditions possible, such as those that exist in solitary retreat. Look for an isolated place where you can find solitude of body, speech and mind. Solitude provides a respite from our hectic, busy lifestyle and freedom from the futile activities that enslave us. Appropriate places are dense forests, vast meadows, high snowy mountains, mountain caves and so on. There, you can make use of outer solitude to develop inner solitude. While you are in retreat, the food you eat and other necessities should be sustained at a normal level. With a completely relaxed mind, develop the practice of shamatha.

During this time, do not live in a group or even in the company of one other person, because that will bring distraction and make one-pointed concentration impossible. The Buddha explained this in the sutras, using the image of a young girl grinding sandalwood. If she is wearing ten different bangles, they will make ten different tinkling sounds. If she is wearing two bangles, they will make a noise as they strike each other. Even if she is wearing only one bangle, it will make a sound as it hits the grinding stone. But if she is not wearing any bracelets at all, there will be no noise. In just the same way, if you are with someone else, there will always be some degree of distraction. Until you develop inner solitude, you have to take advantage of the outer solitude of a place where you can be in peace, free of distractions.

Once you have established yourself in solitude, you need to apply a method to control your mind. Focus on an object such as an image of the Buddha or your personal wisdom deity. While focusing on this object, your mind should be free of three states. It should be free of being withdrawn or submerged, free of being excited or wild, and free of being dull or lazy. Keep your mind completely relaxed.

This third kind of mindfulness, practiced in meditation, is a means of reducing your negative emotions, and when accomplished, it leads you to an understanding of the essence of phenomena. Even this, however, is not enough to address the more subtle defilements and attain complete enlightenment.

This brings us to the fourth kind of mindfulness that the Buddha taught: mindfulness of mind. In practicing mindfulness of mind, the goal is to eliminate self-cherishing. We do this by converting our cherishing of self into cherishing of others. This is the practice known as "exchanging self for others." At first it may be difficult, so we can start with the practice of "equalizing"—treating fellow beings as we would treat ourselves. Just as we ourselves prefer happiness, we should remember that so, too, do all our fellow beings prefer happiness. And just as we dislike suffering, so, too, do all our fellow beings dislike suffering. In the pursuit of happiness and gain, we should work equally hard to attain these riches for fellow beings.

If you undertake the meditative practices for the sole purpose of benefiting yourself, you will not produce any great result. But if you do even one moment of practice for the sake of fellow beings, you will purify the effects of infinite negative actions and will accumulate immeasurable merit. For this reason, whenever you meditate, you should generate bodhicitta. This altruistic motivation called bodhicitta, the mind that is set on enlightenment, can be described as love and compassion. To distill this even further, we can say that bodhicitta means having a good and noble mind. As is said:

> If one has a good and noble mind, then one's journey on the path of dharma will go well.
> If one has a negative state of mind, then one will falter.
> Anything and everything depends on one's mind.
> Therefore, always cultivate a good and noble mind.

Once you have made some progress in the practice of equalizing (seeing the sameness of self and others), you should turn to the practice of exchanging self for others. The practice of equalizing is inadequate in the long run because it still involves self-cherishing. In developing noble mind, or bodhicitta, we must cherish fellow beings even more than we cherish ourselves. All the buddhas and bodhisattvas of this eon generated bodhicitta in this way and eventually attained ultimate buddhahood. Without generating bodhicitta, it is impossible to attain enlightenment. But once bodhicitta blossoms, whatever activity you undertake becomes part of the path leading to enlightenment. It is said in Shantideva's *Bodhicaryavatara* that if you possess bodhicitta, regardless of what you do, you accumulate merit, even while sleeping.

Relative bodhicitta is the desire to attain buddhahood in order to liberate all beings from cyclic existence. It involves keeping the vows and engaging in the practices, and it is a vehicle for attaining absolute bodhicitta. Absolute bodhicitta is emptiness, the direct experience of ultimate truth. As Arya Avalokiteshvara said to the arhat Shariputra, "All entities are empty by nature," meaning that their essence is emptiness. This emptiness is not created by anyone, nor is it something invented by the mind. True emptiness is not a concept. If it were a concept, it would be within the realm of relative truth. If we create concepts, descriptions or mental constructs concerning emptiness, we are only fooling ourselves. With the true realization of emptiness, all fabrications fall away. Not looking back to the past or forward to the future, remain in the present moment. This is mindfulness of mind.

With great aspiration, you have requested teachings from me and the great masters whose words are included in this book. Although it would be impossible to teach this subject in its entirety, I have given a condensed explanation and have now completed my talk. Your request was made with great aspiration, and I too have given this teaching with great aspiration.

In conclusion, the root is bodhicitta. If you are able to generate it, bodhicitta will be the cause of every happiness for yourself and others, and all the suffering you encounter in your daily life will be dispelled. Whether we and our fellow beings experience happiness or suffering, whether we have peace or violence in the world, depends entirely on the condition of our minds. The mind is what determines whether there will be happiness or suffering; our states of mind are what make our actions negative or positive. Therefore, may those who have not already generated this excellent and precious noble mind work very hard to develop it. May those who have already generated bodhicitta try their best not to impair it, working hard to increase love and compassion so that it continues to grow.

Our awareness of bodhicitta depends completely on the existence of the Buddhist teachings. So we must pray to the Buddha for the perpetuation of the Buddhadharma and its holders, such as His Holiness the Dalai Lama and the other great teachers. May they live long, and may their work of disseminating the Buddha's teachings remain unhampered. Throughout this wide world, may there be timely rain and sunshine; may harvests be abundant and everyone prosperous. In conclusion, may all sentient beings cease their negative actions and be free of suffering, may they all enjoy well-being and happiness, and ultimately may all beings attain buddhahood.

KHANDRO TSERING CHÖDRÖN

Meeting

KHANDRO TSERING CHÖDRÖN

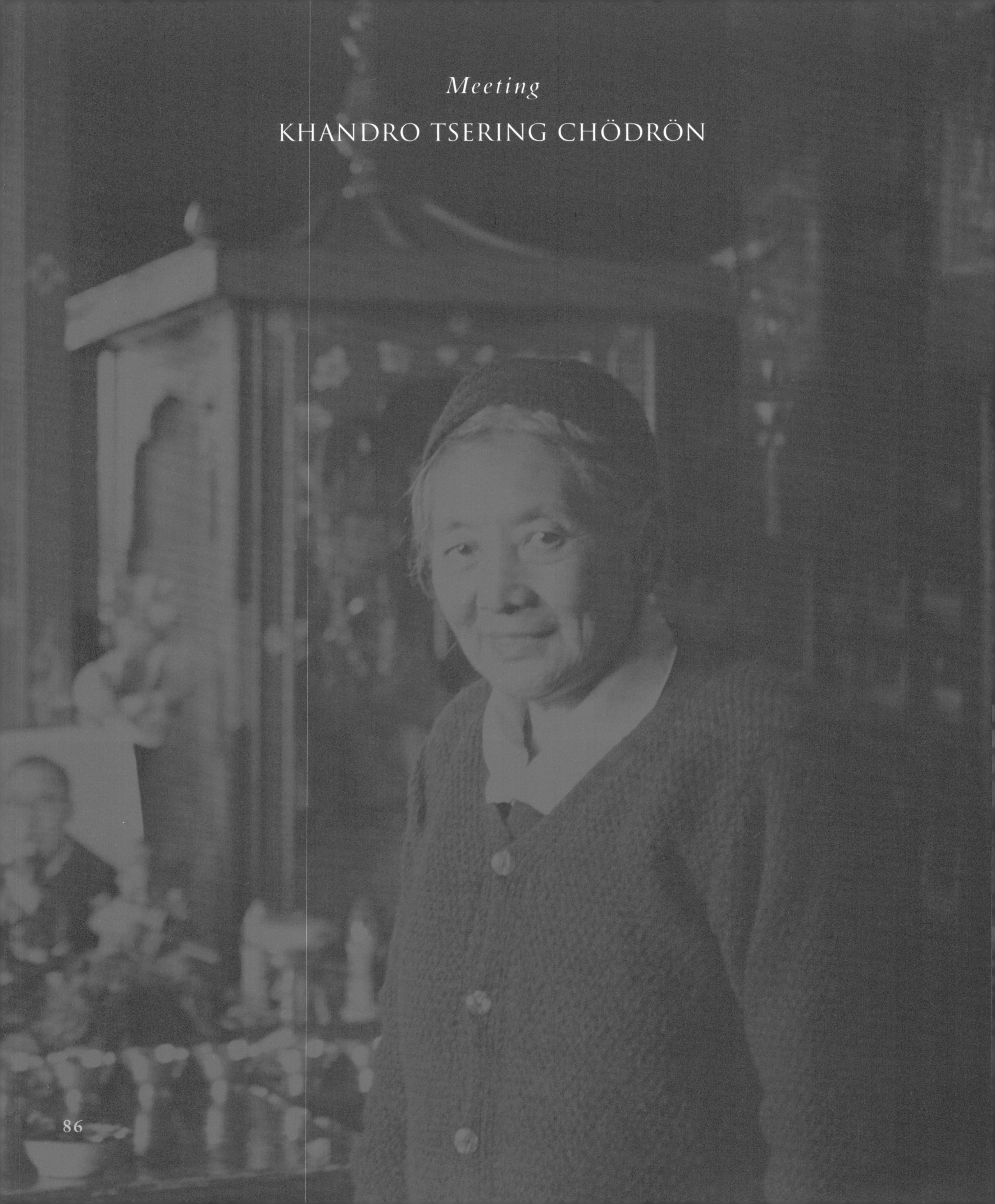

I FIRST MET THE ESTEEMED KHANDRO TSERING CHÖDRÖN while Dungsey Thinley Norbu Rinpoche was visiting our home in Boudhanath. When she came to see Rinpoche, he motioned me to his side and whispered, "There is a great dakini in the house—she has just walked into the sitting room. You can offer a katak and make three full prostrations at her feet. She is the khandro of the great Jamyang Khyentse Chökyi Lodrö. When you see her face, you see the face of a true dakini." Rinpoche's words echoed in my mind each time I saw Khandro Tsering thereafter.

Two decades later, Penzom Lama and I traveled to Sikkim to seek teachings from Khandro for this book. She lives quietly in a temple set on the expansive grounds of the Sikkimese Royal Palace. We walked to the deep crimson door of the temple, slid off our shoes and tiptoed into the entry hall to find her attendant. He guided us to the dimly lit shrine room where Khandro Tsering stood, her serene radiance illuminating the shadows. Seeing her was like being embraced by a divine love, her presence the breathing essence of faith. She gestured to us, and with gentle Tibetan words asked us to sit and take tea. We would speak intermittently and then the conversation would change naturally to silent meditation as we sat in front of the reliquary of her guru, Jamyang Khyentse Chökyi Lodrö. Eventually I made my request for a teaching. Khandro replied that she didn't teach but that we could include her picture here along with the words of Jamyang Khyentse Chökyi Lodrö.

It was not easy for me to leave that day. Being in such a holy atmosphere was indescribably moving, and I wanted to stay there forever. As we walked out, my heart felt washed of pain and full of love. May these photos bring Khandro Tsering's presence here, and may the advice of Khyentse Chökyi Lodrö release the hearts of all who read his sacred words.

JAMYANG KHYENTSE CHÖKYI LODRÖ

My Vital Advice

Homage to the unsurpassed savior, the Lord of Oddiyana.

Now that you've found this precious human life with freedom and richness,
Take care not to squander it unconsciously.
Push yourself to uncover the meaning of this life.

Your mind is the source of everything.
It is skilled in deception and manipulation, and beguiling when unexamined.
Once you look into it, it is without basis or root.
It comes from nowhere, stays nowhere and goes nowhere.
Everything, including samsara and nirvana,
Is but a reflection of pure and impure mind;
In reality, neither samsara nor nirvana exist.

The source of compassionate awareness
Is primordially empty. Though free from characteristics,
It is not just a barren nothingness
But is luminous and naturally present.

Pristine awareness is not captured by names and labels.
The endless unfolding of samsara and nirvana pours forth as its radiance.
At the same time, there is no rift between the place from where all these come
  and that which is coming;
Remain in that nondual place.

Unborn dharmakaya Rigpa
Arises naturally without cause or condition.
Alert, fresh and naked,
It is uncolored by dualistic mind
And unpolluted by intellectual ideas.
Stay in that spontaneously arisen meditation.
Even the words "to meditate" are but words;

In reality, there is no meditator and nothing to meditate on.
Without distraction, always maintain empty awareness,
The true face of dharmakaya.

The deluded karma of samsara will never run out.
The more you work to solve your problems, the greater they become.
Belief in enemies and friends grows and grows,
And the causes for incarnating in lower realms pile up.
Direct yourself toward the dharma,
And if you can bring dharma to every action, word and thought,
You will uncover the great awakening, the path to liberation.
When death falls upon you, you will regret nothing.
During this life and in those to come,
You will walk the path of ever-growing happiness.

Atop your head and in your heart,
Imagine as a single being
Your most kind guru and the great Lord of Oddiyana.
Feel an upwelling of unbearable longing and devotion.
Whatever joy or sorrow befalls you, whatever favor or misfortune,
Pray forever to the lord Guru.
Let your minds flow together, yours at one with his.

As death draws near, let go of all attachment and hatred.
Picture Guru Padmasambhava above your head;
Imagine your consciousness as an orb of light, marked with the syllable *Hri;*
Dissolve that into the heart of the guru.
If you practice regularly now
And recite "The Aspiration to Be Born in the Copper-Colored Mountain,"
At death, a clear visualization will be easy.

To put it briefly, the essence of dharma
Is to cut through clinging to samsara,
To cultivate love and compassion toward those in the six realms
And to completely tame one's mind.
Without distraction, please always practice thus.

Even though I am immune to dharma, have no experience of meditation, and just use up the donations, I, Chökyi Lodrö, wrote this according to what the past masters have taught, to fulfill the request of the yogini Pad Lu.

NYOSHUL KHENPO RINPOCHE

Meeting

NYOSHUL KHENPO RINPOCHE

I FIRST SAW THE GREAT DZOGCHEN MASTER NYOSHUL KHENPO RINPOCHE IN 1984. He was sitting in a garden outside Dilgo Khyentse Rinpoche's home in Dordogne, gazing into the blue above. Rinpoche had an air of bliss and stillness, and I remember thinking he looked as if he were master of the sky.

One night, there was a dinner gathering at our small stone farmhouse, and Rinpoche honored us by attending. Fortunate as the occasion was, I remember that evening with some embarrassment. None of the guests at the table spoke fluent English, and we were at a loss as to how to entertain Rinpoche, so after dinner we asked my teenage daughter to sing for him. She reluctantly brought out her guitar and played the one melody she remembered the words to—a ballad about a prostitute called "House of the Rising Sun." I listened with the blood rushing to my face as she crooned the song, lamenting the miseries of life in a brothel. I was the only discomfited listener; Khen Rinpoche knew no English and seemed to enjoy the performance. When I later asked my daughter, "How could you have sung that song?" she answered, "You mean the one about the sun?"

I next encountered Rinpoche a year later, shortly after our return to California. We were living in a tiny vacation rental dwarfed by the expansive Pacific Ocean out front. The house was not more than twelve feet wide, with plywood walls, a galley kitchen and two closet-sized bedrooms upstairs. A friend from a local Buddhist center called one day and asked that we host Rinpoche, since all the rental houses in the area were filled. So, to our good fortune, Khen Rinpoche and his wife, Khandro Damcho, ended up staying with us for a few weeks in that boxcar by the sea.

Rinpoche enjoyed taking walks along the ocean, and we would often follow. He spoke little, but would gesture up to the empty cerulean heaven, breathing it in deeply and urging us to do the same. Walking with Rinpoche felt like stepping right into the clear sky. He communicated to the world with his poetic speech, graceful gestures and quiet eyes. Each person he met he greeted as a beloved friend, instantly opening the hearts of all who saw him.

During those weeks, I asked Rinpoche if he would give a teaching for this book. He asked that I use one of his poems or letters instead, and I chose a missive he wrote to his disciples in 1981. This is only one of the many beautiful poems that the illustrious Nyoshul Khenpo Rinpoche left as part of his legacy. The profound teachings, poems and kindness of this great master of Dzogchen live on for us all.

NYOSHUL KHENPO RINPOCHE

The Song of Illusion

HOMAGE TO THE GURU!

Illusory wisdom reflection of Drimé Öser,

Inseparable from Jampel Pawo, only father of all the Buddhas,

Who manifested in this decadent age to guide beings to liberation,

O, my root teacher, Tenpai Nyima, you know all things!

Self-arisen Dharma lord, show the undeluded nature of the mind

To those who through delusion are deceived by false appearances.

Kye Ho! Listen carefully, fortunate friends,

Swans dwelling on the glorious summer lake of the Buddha's doctrine!

To my disciples and *vajra* brothers and sisters long known to me,

I offer a spontaneous letter to tell you how I am, a song of illusion.

Do not think it is wrong of me to express myself openly,

But listen well to it, the playful friend of your golden lotus ears.

Although in this life I possess no great qualities,

Through the perfect merit of pure actions previously accumulated,

I met the incomparable lama, jewel of the sky.

With faith like a lake of stainless milk, white on the surface and below,

I exerted myself in serving my spiritual friend, the root of all Dharma.

And just as, at the foot of a mountain of precious gold,

Even ordinary pebbles are tinted with its radiance,

So too my mind—trapped in the net of discursive thoughts, fettered by common delusion,

The spiked iron chains of intense duality and clinging to solidity—found rest.

A beggar, free from activity, relaxed in a happy, open state of mind,

I destroyed the web of the eight worldly concerns of illusory hopes and fears.

The king of Dharma, Longchen Rabjam, said,

"Activities are endless, like ripples on a stream,

They end when we leave them: such is their nature."

So too, through the kindness of the lama who taught me non-activity and self-appearance,

The thought arose in me that without doing anything, everything is accomplished.

In front there is no one I need to protect: a *yogin,* I am happy!

Behind, no one to sustain: alone, I am joyful!

I have no work to put off: with no time lost, I am happy!

I have no use for long-term plans: relaxed, I am joyful!

Criticized, I am not depressed: undismayed, I am happy!

Through the kindness of the lama who showed me the great middle path,

As Buddha taught, not swayed by either extreme of life's necessities,

Though I sleep in a lovely mansion of the finest gold,

Overflowing with heaps of various jewels,

I have no need to be haughty or seek admiration.

Though I dwell in cool shady gardens of fruit trees, the excellent refuge of the lower man,

Or huts of latticed grass,

I have no need for lament. My mind is not seized by hopes and fears.

Through the kindness of the teacher who taught me the pre-eminence of the supreme *bodhi*-mind,

I remain loving and kind to whoever I meet, high or low,

Man or woman, my parents from long ago.

I treat them all as close brothers and sisters, with love in my heart.

For this the stupid and jealous may mock me,

But they cannot change my naturally kind thoughts.

To the man in the street I am careless and childish, whatever happens.

"He is an aimless wanderer. He gives no importance to wealth," they may say.

But distracted by accumulating and protecting this ground of all suffering, destruction, and quarrel,

One cuts the vital vein of the virtuous mind,

And one's human life is carried away like paper in the wind:

So I do not cherish much this weapon to kill myself!

Through the kindness of the lama who taught me that there is no need for anything,

I do not hope to quench my thirst with the mirage-water of the eight worldly concerns.

Since prejudiced praise and blame are like the sound of an echo,

And the human mind like the sun's rays on a snowcapped mountain,

Expecting nothing from inferiors, I am not tied to a retinue.

I do not try to catch the colors of the rainbow through not understanding its nature,

And even if others do not like me, my mind is happy.

Through the kindness of the lama who introduced me to the wisdom bliss of the fulfillment stage,
I took the support of the wisdom consort, the messenger of skillful means:
The taste of great bliss, milked from the cow of the sky,
Sealed the aggregates, elements, sense consciousnesses, and all things, the universe and beings,
And all appearances arose as the symbol of great bliss.
Happy am I, a yogin enjoying the four joys of great bliss!

Through the kindness of the lama who introduced me to all things as illusions,
Appearance was revealed as unobstructed and evanescent in the endless wheel of illusion,
Sound as the clear and unborn notes of an echo,
And aimless discursive thoughts arising of themselves, and dispersing and vanishing like clouds.

Kye Ho! Friends! Look at this wonderful show!
In the plain of the absolute nature, from the first, beyond bondage and freedom,
The son of a barren woman riding the elephant of illusion,
His head adorned with a sky-flower, comes dancing and singing!
Who imposed the pattern of the theories of discursive thought
On phenomenal existence, the manifest dance of the kingly *dharmakaya*?
How wonderful is this illusory show of samsara and nirvana!

As the kind teacher who introduced me to the absolute nature as illusion declared,
"In the primordial wisdom-space, free from dust, pure and all-pervading,
The realization of the unbiased absolute body is free from falling into extremes.
What use is meditation that clings to concrete reality and hopes and fears?"

Even if one remains ordinary, not meditating, who is deluded?
How wonderful is the sky-like yoga of the nonactivity of the absolute nature!
The childish, clinging to concrete reality, boast about doing things where there is nothing to do.
They are like thirsty deer trying to reach the water of a mirage.
Poor ignorant creatures, tormented by pointless fatigue!
Through the kindness of the teacher who showed me appearance and activity as illusion,
When the myriad colored lights of samsara and nirvana,
The self-radiant and unobstructed play of the wisdom of the absolute space,
Arose in the land of illusion as the play of illusion,
The illusory yogin reached the self-domain of illusion.

What use to him are these illusory dreamlike appearances,
Empty, hollow and without essence, like bamboo,
Insubstantial forms like a moon in water, like visions in the air?

Through the kindness of the teacher who revealed all appearance as illusion,
The mist of the discursive judgements of intellectual analysis
And intense attraction to illusory things, dissolved in self-liberation,
In the absolute space which is birthless, beyond thought and expression.
No more bondage of hope and fear!
No more bondage of adopting and rejection!

Ema! Listen well, dear friends!
Although I am neither shrewd nor clever, this is what I think:
In essence, when the illusory yogin has exhausted acceptance and rejection,
Samsara and nirvana arise as an illusory play.
This indeed is the fruit itself, free from all obscurations.
Apart from this, what use is great knowledge and understanding?

Through the kindness of the teacher, the incomparable glorious protector, who spoke all this,
I received this legacy of Longchen Rabjam's instructions,
Which is impossible to evaluate in gold and jewels.
Although I think I might, in this mere intellectual way, point towards
The realization of the heart-essence of luminous absolute space,
I have not gained the slightest experience of it, not to mention any realization.
If I have made mistakes, I confess them to the *yidams* and teachers.

As the lord of the world, Drimé Öser, said,
"Disciples and vajra brothers and sisters long known to me,
Now, when you have the support of the wish-fulfilling jewel endowed with freedom and riches,
And the Buddha's doctrine is radiating like a snow mountain in its youthful splendor,
All of you, like lion cubs in the prime of youth,
Follow the Buddha, the lion among men!

After bringing experiences and realization to perfection, like the snow lion's abundant turquoise mane,
You will soon reach the kingdom of the blissful absolute expanse!"

Even if I, an evil doer, go to hell one day,
I am sure to have the fortune of being freed by the gracious lama,
And I wish and pray that at that time all beings who had a connection with me
May enjoy unsurpassable enlightenment
In the beautiful blue lotus buddha-field of the *Tathagata*.
Until then I pray that by the power of relative karma,
We vajra brothers and sisters may meet again and again,
And enjoy the secret teaching of the omniscient teacher, Longchenpa,
The ambrosia of the heart-treasure of luminosity.
Moreover, to you the *sangha*, worthy of worship by gods and men,
I offer a white *pundarika* flower, and a prayer:
May your lotus feet remain for oceans of *kalpas*,
And may the myriad light rays of the teaching and practice of Dharma
Radiate in a hundred directions.

Though self-awareness, the kingly doer of all, is beyond movement and effort,
These words, sincere bearers of my news, are its self-manifestation, the dancing song of
   the mind's child:
They came from the palace of the deep red tent within the breast,
In the great mountain citadel of the body,
Through the secret way of the sixteen-petalled enjoyment *chakra*,
Sent on a path of white paper as dazzling as a snowy mountain,
To the monastery of Namling Shedrub in the Sandalwood Forest.

DZONGSAR JAMYANG KHYENTSE RINPOCHE

Meeting

DZONGSAR JAMYANG KHYENTSE RINPOCHE

My FIRST GLIMPSE OF DZONGSAR KHYENTSE RINPOCHE is still engraved on my mind. He had come to Kathmandu to visit his father, Dungsey Thinley Norbu Rinpoche, and he walked purposefully into our little cement house dressed in yellow robes. As he turned to meet his father, Khyentse Rinpoche adjusted his golden zen, snapping it from his shoulders and into the air behind him in a wide arc. The sun filtered through the cotton as it floated back down, washing the small room in saffron light. Rinpoche's posture was straight and regal, and his stride light and very long. In that moment, I felt as though Prince Siddhartha had just walked through the room.

At seventeen, Rinpoche was already well versed in English. Nevertheless, he took all his studies very seriously and would call me to the monastery to help him refine his grammar and vocabulary. During the lessons, his attendant would come and go, invariably showing up just when Rinpoche needed something. Rinpoche would make a quick motion with his hand in a vague direction; then, without needing an explanation, the monk would hurry to one of the low cushions lined up against the walls. Reaching under one of the pillows, he would retrieve whatever item Rinpoche had nonverbally requested, always seeming to know exactly what Rinpoche wanted and where it would be. Many things were concealed under those seats; his letters, an envelope filled with rupees, English books, Tintin comics and extra socks were all kept in this unique filing system. It was the only thing that reminded me of the youth of this great incarnation of Jamyang Khyentse Chökyi Lodrö, holder of the Rimé (nonsectarian) tradition. Rinpoche's brilliance and recall made the lessons almost unnecessary, but I loved pretending to tutor him.

Many years passed, and we eventually left the peaceful land of Nepal. We were reluctant to go. That pocket in the Himalayas was a place where Hindus and Buddhists lived easily side by side, often sharing their temples. Kathmandu was a place where cows took afternoon siestas in the middle of the street while imperturbable rickshaw drivers maneuvered carefully around them. It was a place where respect for the spiritual was evident in every aspect of daily life, and when we returned to the United States we dearly missed our old home.

Shortly after we had moved back to California in 1986, my daughter Kitty picked up the phone one day to the distant sound of an overseas connection. The voice on the phone was Dzongsar Khyentse Rinpoche. He said that he would be coming to the United States soon, so we requested that he stay at our home. He began to visit periodically after that.

Much in the manner of a renaissance man, Rinpoche was interested in everything—science, literature, communication, art. Our discussions sometimes centered on communication through artistic media, particularly photography and film. This piqued my interest since I had long felt that the visual arts access the unconscious mind and have the capacity to communicate in ways that words and concepts cannot. Rinpoche's own photographs had this effect; whatever image he chose—faces, flowers, stones—their soulful beauty invited me to linger.

On some days, several Buddhist students would be sitting in the living room talking with Rinpoche when suddenly he would turn on some music—perhaps Beethoven or Ravi Shankar. He would say, "Shh, listen!" and then turn the volume to its highest level so that music rode through the whole house. Then, abruptly, he would turn the volume down and return to the conversation. Those interludes seemed to disrupt the flow of discursive thought for one expansive moment.

One afternoon during Rinpoche's first visit to Santa Cruz, the doorbell rang, and I opened the door to find two Jehovah's Witnesses. Walking up behind me, Rinpoche quickly invited them in for tea. He didn't tell the two clean-cut young men that he was Buddhist, but their blue eyes grew wide as they walked into our living room filled with pictures of Guru Rinpoche and Buddhist deities. Rinpoche spent more than an hour talking with the pair, listening with interest to their message of conversion and graciously accepting literature from their church.

Rinpoche stayed with us for only a week during that first visit, but the blessing of his presence continued as the Jehovah's Witnesses knocked on our door week after week. In fact, they still come. And although Rinpoche now sometimes dresses in maroon robes and sometimes in London-made wool coats, I still see him as the Buddha.

DZONGSAR JAMYANG KHYENTSE RINPOCHE

Inhibitions, Conservativeness and Taboos

FOR THIS BOOK I WANT TO TALK ABOUT INHIBITIONS, conservativeness and taboos and how these alienate us from our own basic goodness, our buddha nature.

All beings have buddha nature. Nothing can improve upon it, nothing can destabilize it. Stainless from the beginning, its radiance cannot be corrupted. Though we all have the essence of Buddha, the wrapping of emotions, habitual patterns, inhibitions and the like temporarily obscures it. To use an analogy, think of soiled cloth: the dirt is not inherent in the cloth, but until we wash the fabric, its true nature is disguised. Everyone accepts that clothes are washable, that the dirt is impermanent. We know the clothes were clean when we bought them; the bill didn't say "shirt $25, tax $5, dirt $10." The very reason we spend money on things like soap and washing machines is that we trust the dirt is temporal and can be washed away. And furthermore, we have the motivation to put the clothes in the washing machine, add the soap and wash them.

Similarly, at the highest levels of Buddhism, you accept your intrinsic buddha nature. You accept that there is a way to eliminate temporal dirt by practicing the dharma, and you also accept that obscurations can be removed. My own grandmother and mother washed their clothes, and they came out clean. It worked. My masters and their masters practiced the dharma and have done this for thousands of years—taken the path, washed themselves and reached the ultimate nature. Stains are removable. Yet after all this time, I myself still have not realized the power of the statement "The stain is removable." That stains are removable is the essence of the Buddhist path.

All the seeming negativity and troubles in your life are a result of cause and condition. They are not "God given"; they are not in your true nature. Nor do they occur by chance. It is not like you smell dog shit from across the street and out of the blue some appears on your shoe. You have to really step in it. Do you understand what I'm saying? This is actually good news because it means you have the power to manipulate the very causes and conditions which have created your problems. When you eliminate negative causes and conditions, what is left behind is what we call buddha nature.

The inhibitions that obscure our buddha nature develop because we use external points of reference to define and confirm our own self-identity. The problem with this is that reference points continually change. As we try to keep up with these varying references, inhibitions build upon themselves and multiply. Our self-consciousness increases, and we experience fear and

vulnerability. Reference points are the cause of our hope, fear and inhibitions, and they take us farther and farther from our buddha nature. So you might as well cut inhibitions and go back to what is true—your own basic goodness, your buddha nature.

> *Rinpoche, the use of the word "inhibition" here is confusing to me.*
> *Can you please explain it further?*

At the root of our inhibitions are habitual patterns. Habitual patterns are the cause and inhibitions are the result. We've accumulated countless inhibitions and taboos throughout our many lifetimes. Consider how many we've collected just in this life—from our education, society, family, friends, as Americans, as Chinese, as Russians. We have managed to create some quite amazing belief systems as well as institutions to support them. For example, some people refer to *Vogue* and *Esquire* to decide what constitutes a beautiful body. They may decide that they are too thin or too fat, their breasts are the wrong size, or they have too little hair. To transform themselves, they can go to a plastic surgeon who spent years in medical school; they can buy some special undergarment with lots of straps; they can get a toupee or a hair transplant. There are endless possibilities. Inhibitions are a big business, by the way.

> *Rinpoche, what would happen if we didn't have inhibitions? Wouldn't life become messy and chaotic?*
> *Wouldn't shedding our inhibitions make us even more selfish?*

As you shed inhibitions, you become more and more genuine. But be careful here! That doesn't mean you become some sort of "rebel without a cause" or New Age flower child. It doesn't mean you trade in your current inhibitions for more outrageous ones. Nor does it mean that you express your emotions indiscriminately. It is much more profound than that. Destroying inhibitions actually has beneficial side effects. You may no longer care what people think. Whether you receive criticism or praise, you are detached from it because you know that criticism and praise would only fuel further inhibitions. A lack of inhibitions is beneficial because you are able to empathize with others. When people are moody, annoying or difficult, you can think, "Ah, this is caused by their inhibitions." You will have compassion, just as a doctor has sympathy for a mental patient who is unaware of his own illness.

> *Rinpoche, if I were free of inhibitions in the way you've described, how would I respond*
> *if I saw a father angrily beating his child?*

The teachings of Shantideva answer your question succinctly: it is not the person; it is the anger. Because the father himself is a victim of his own rage, your antagonism would be directed

toward his anger, not toward him. So, so beautiful. Shantideva…my god, he was a great man! It's amazing such beings have actually existed on this earth. Is there some sort of retroactive Nobel Peace Prize? They should give it to Shantideva, don't you think?

Yes, Rinpoche, I agree. When I hear the words "inhibition" and "taboo," I think of a superficial kind of behavior or self-consciousness, but when I think about karmic patterns, I imagine them to be much more subtle and to run deeper. To what extent are habitual patterns, inhibitions and taboos related to karma?

Very much so—everything is karma. As long as there is mind, there is karma. Nothing is "non-karma," sadly. Our habitual patterns and karma are like the question of the chicken and the egg. Habitual patterns are both the cause of future karma and the result of past karma. There are certain inhibitions we possess that appear to have no basis in culture or environment. This is where Freud was mistaken. Without a belief in past lives, we must find the cause of our problems in this one, and often blame is assigned—to the parents, the difficult childhood, the dysfunctional relationships, society and so on. But actually we should realize that there are many lifetimes. And some of our current inhibitions, conservativeness and taboos are not a product of this life but are in fact a continuation of past karmic patterns.

Rinpoche, if both personal and societal inhibitions are so pervasive and influential, how can we ever overcome them? In fact, how can we even begin to recognize them?

By meditation. By not stirring.

Not stirring? How?

Sit straight…thoughts come…just watch…don't do anything…don't suppress…don't encourage. If you don't stir muddy water, it will become clear on its own. If you stir muddy water, it will become even murkier. So just let it be. The inhibitions will eventually settle down. If you are not a practitioner, it will take some time. As you practice a little bit every day, gradually the positive effects will accumulate. That's why we do daily practice.

Thank you, Rinpoche. The other day you also spoke about alertness being the key to disengaging from our inhibitions. I'm not sure what you mean by "alertness."

Not stirring is alertness. Meditation is alertness. By staying alert, you avoid falling into fakeness, a lack of authenticity. But keep in mind—alertness is not a goal or result in and of itself. Alertness is a path. Alertness is a tool. You must strive to be alert all the time so that you avoid the two hindrances on the path. The first of these is "mistaken path," and it occurs when you begin to think that there is no cause and condition, no past life, no Buddha. Then you have fallen from the path.

The second hindrance is "sidetracked path," where the path itself is the problem. Those who have made progress are actually much more susceptible to being sidetracked. For instance, they might get bored with the path and be diverted to another, perhaps for hundreds of lifetimes. Or then again, they might become so consumed with a certain aspect of the path that they impede their own progress. For example, humility is a virtue. But if you fixate on the idea that in order to be virtuous you must be humble, then it can become a hindrance, because sometimes to truly benefit others you must use the opposite of humility. If a baby is moving toward a fire, it isn't skillful to speak humbly and gently; you have to say, "No!" forcefully. It is similar to the way a Surrealistic painting by Miró might resonate more powerfully with someone than a beautiful still life of fruit by Cézanne.

Some individuals can also be sidetracked if they walk on the path and attain a certain level, but enjoy it so much that they stop there and don't continue. They have fallen in love with the path itself and forgotten their destination. These hindrances can occur, so it's very important to use alertness—as a method, as a tool, as a guard.

Rinpoche, do you think some people might misinterpret "overcoming inhibitions"
as a way to justify careless behavior?

That's interesting. Ego dwells in the inhibitions. In the process of trying to eliminate one immediate inhibition, you develop another inhibition. This happens to many so-called spiritual people. Becoming attached to freedom from inhibition is just creating an additional hang-up, so it's not freedom. Do you understand? If I tell you, "You are beautiful," you won't take it seriously. But if I say, "Something is wrong with your lips," you will imbue my words with great meaning and think about them for days, won't you? Selective listening is a very human trait, and often we pick and choose from the teachings according to what is most comfortable or according to our already established inhibitions. But that is why our path is not working. It is very important that when we decide to take Buddha seriously, we take everything he says seriously.

How do we eliminate inhibitions without violating the basic principles of humanity?
It seems there are some principles we should keep.

We have many principles, don't we? But principles are mind-made. They can change from day to day and are a product of reference, education and whatever values you have adopted. There is no such thing as "original principles." The problem is, as long as you cling to one principle, you are stuck. For now, you don't have to banish all of them, but be aware that principles are just ideas, not a fixed ethic. From a spiritual point of view, all these principles will eventually have to go. The tricky thing is this: though our aim should be eliminating all inhibitions and principles, in order to do that, we must temporarily adopt certain principles and nourish certain inhibitions as a method on the path.

So it seems we have to fabricate to a certain extent, and yet we're supposed to be rescuing the "unfabricated." How do we balance these two?

You don't need to balance them. Actually, the unfabricated needs to take over anyway.

Rinpoche, I'm still worried about being genuine. If we didn't hold back to a certain extent, then what we think, what we feel or what we experience would surely disrupt others.

What makes you think you would disrupt other people by being genuine? You would not. That's not what I mean by "uninhibited." Being authentic would increase your respect for others. You would know they are suffering because they are not being genuine themselves. You would respond to them naturally with courteous, careful compassion, without the slightest taint of arrogance. You would empathize with their vulnerabilities and act appropriately with true kindness. Do you see?

It is very difficult to convey what it means to have no inhibitions. But Dzogchen masters express it as a child's experience from the adult's point of view. For instance, children, and babies in particular, are not apprehensive about being naked. They are neither afraid nor courageous about it. Do you understand? There is no fear but also no absence of fear. As adults, we would be quite embarrassed to stroll through the streets naked. But that is an inhibition we have developed. It is not innate.

Dzogchen, the Great Perfection, is definitely the destroyer of inhibition. So perhaps we should close here with the words of my grandfather, Kyabje Dudjom Rinpoche:

> Buddhahood is not attained by fabricated dharmas.
> Meditation made by the mind, fabricated by the intellect, is the deceiving enemy.
> Now, clinging to style and manner is destroyed with crazy abandon.
> Let this life be spent in the state of uninhibited naked ease!

CHAGDUD TULKU RINPOCHE

Meeting

CHAGDUD TULKU RINPOCHE

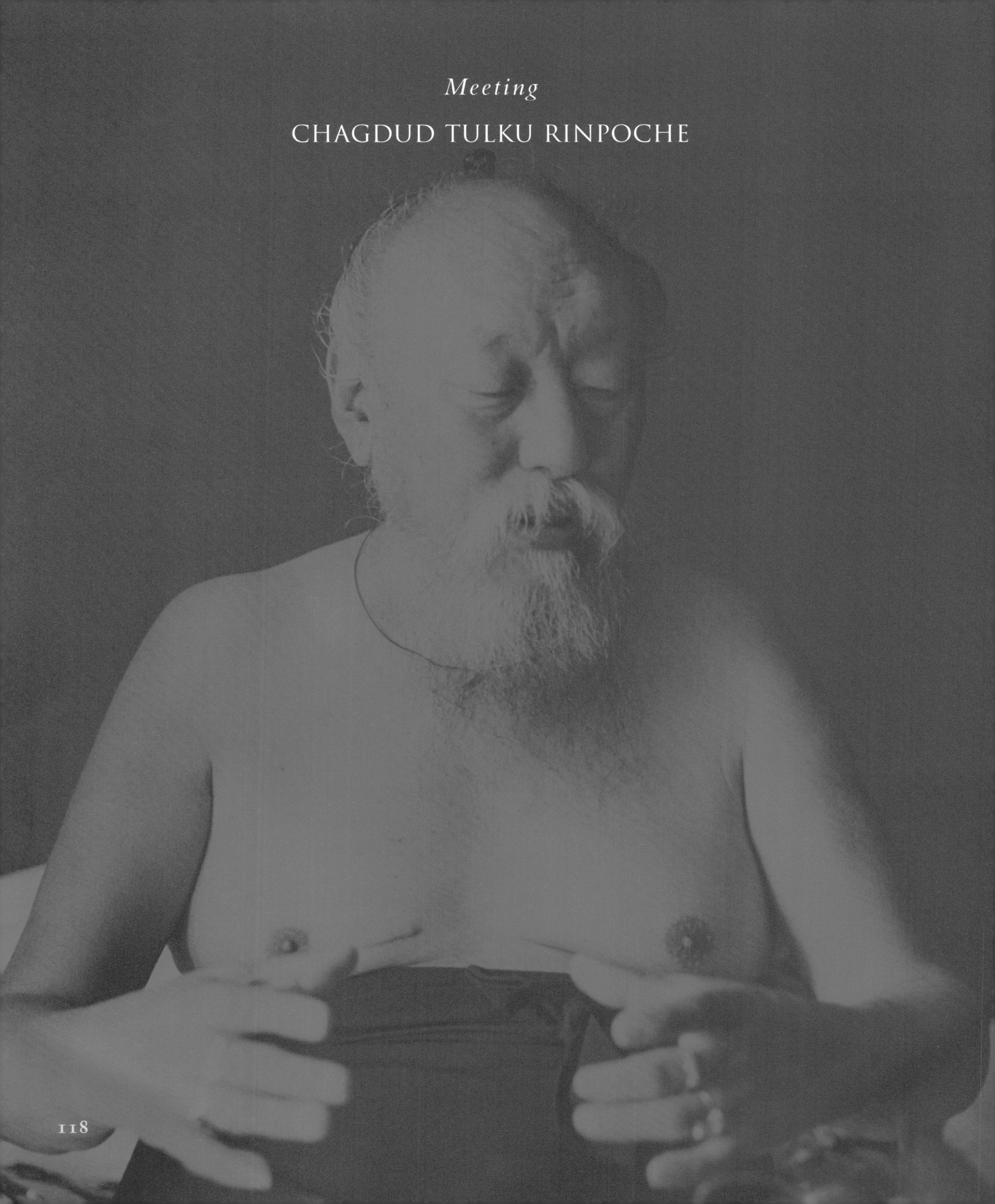

ᴇARLY IN 1978, a friend took me to meet Chagdud Tulku Rinpoche, who was living in Kathmandu at the time. We walked through Boudhanath, stepping around the old Brahma bull with a twisted horn who spent his leisurely days languishing in the middle of the road. As we approached Rinpoche's house, a melodious chant drifted from the windows, filling the street with the sound of his beautiful voice—a sound that has drawn me ever since. When we entered the room, Rinpoche was sitting on a narrow bed, his long black hair piled in a topknot like the siddhas' of old, eyes partially closed as he sang. A rapt group of Tibetans sat crowded together on the floor, faces soft with delight as they listened. Rinpoche was singing folksongs, the stories of old Tibet woven in velvet tones. The room was steeped in warmth and happiness, and all those who came, including first-time visitors like myself, were greeted as old friends.

The only other Westerner present was a light-haired woman dressed in a faded black Tibetan dress. We spoke while she made tea for Rinpoche's visitors using a rickety kerosene burner, and I learned that she had been living near the remote caves of Tsopema, a holy place of Guru Rinpoche. She had just recently come back to Kathmandu. I was perplexed and stared at her blankly as she spoke, wondering how this clearly refined woman could possibly live as a recluse in the rugged mountains of northern India. Her name was Jane, and she soon became my dear friend.

It seemed as though Jane worked unceasingly. From dawn until late into the night, she practiced, studied, cooked, listened to teachings and helped Rinpoche in whatever way she could. She had the strangest attitude. Instead of noticing how much she had accomplished or dwelling on how tired she was, Jane would speak about how she hadn't done enough for Rinpoche and how she must do better. Although I didn't know it then, she had the attitude one reads about in stories of great devotees but is quite rare to see.

In those days, Jane and I would go for tea in one of the dungeon-like restaurants of Boudhanath, ducking to enter through low carved doors built to fit Nepalese. We would sit and talk in the cramped darkness, eating dumplings called momos and sipping chai. Jane would be perfectly poised, somewhat enigmatic, always incredibly funny and insightful. She spoke like an intellectual from New York and dressed like a Tibetan from Kham. Even sitting there in a teashop with mud walls, drinking five-cent cups of tea, Jane couldn't help displaying the manners of a queen. She later married Chagdud Rinpoche, and over the years her refinement and manners seemed to overtake every aspect of her life. She worked, practiced and devoted herself completely to him and through his guidance was transformed into an outstanding student, dharma representative and teacher.

Rinpoche and Jane came to the United States in 1979 and established a Buddhist center in a small Oregon town by a river. From this remote place, Rinpoche's dharma activities rapidly expanded. As his students grew in number, centers eventually opened all over the country, from California and New Mexico to New York and Alaska.

Rinpoche gave the Nyingma teachings to thousands of people. Never allowing unfamiliar students to think of the ceremonies associated with practice as mysterious rituals, he explained the power of transformation embedded in every aspect of Vajrayana Buddhism. He clarified and transmitted to his non-Tibetan students the deeper meaning of each offering, hand gesture and ring of the bell. He brought the Nyingma teachings directly to our hearts, heads and hands.

By 1995 Rinpoche's activities in the United States were well established, and he moved to Brazil to be closer to his South American disciples. Seeking his teaching for this book led me to the unexpectedly peaceful southern region of Brazil. One of Rinpoche's students met me at the airport, and we drove to Três Coroas, where his center is located. Accompanied by the muted beat of samba music from the truck's radio, we drove through meandering foothills carpeted in greenery. Each turn of the road brought another low mountain into view as if we were driving through a natural maze. Finally, in the midst of tranquility, Khadro Ling appeared to my impatient eyes like a vivid red jewel. We pulled up behind three large buses filled with Brazilians, and my companion explained that the doors of the temple were always open to visitors. Although these people were tourists, they showed a sincere reverence as they explored the site; Rinpoche often said that many Brazilians have a natural affinity for the spiritual.

As we entered Rinpoche's house above the temple, I saw Jane, now known as Chagdud Khadro, a title of respect given to her by Rinpoche. She was just inside the doorway, waving her finger and scolding a very sweet, fluffy puppy. After greeting me in her gracious way, she served tea and we sat together as we had done so many years before. Khadro spoke about Rinpoche's most recent activities and teachings throughout Brazil and Uruguay. She mentioned that just the night before, he had opened a rock concert with twenty minutes of Tibetan chanting. The audience of forty thousand was enraptured by his voice just as the Tibetans had been the day I first met him.

Chagdud Khadro took me to Rinpoche. Around us, a constant stream of people moved in and out of Rinpoche's house as they worked on an array of projects—translating Buddhist texts, making statues and tormas, sewing text covers. There was no room in his home that wasn't filled with the constant buzz of dharma work in progress, and I felt a sense of déjà vu. I had to remind myself that I wasn't in Nepal, Oregon or California. The Brazilian students were unfailingly kind and polite, as are the students at all Chagdud Gonpa centers.

The tiny white poodle had the run of the house. She scampered from room to room, periodically searching for Rinpoche and stretching out in his lap like a human child. Rinpoche had a special love of dogs, and his centers were often filled with newly rescued animals. Rehabilitated strays would be nursed back to health and spend contented days following Rinpoche around before being adopted by his students.

No matter where I met Rinpoche, whether in a small cement room in Nepal, the lush forests of Oregon, or a traditional Buddhist temple set in the Brazilian hills, he carried the same constantly expanding sphere of love and dharma activity. His care and compassion for everyone who came to him always seemed to yield the comfort of a practical solution. In the face of my own or others' anguish, he offered the enveloping kindness a person would expect only from her own mother.

Now I think back to the weeks in Brazil with longing and gratitude, since these teachings were the last I received from Rinpoche. When the preparation of this chapter began, Chagdud Tulku Rinpoche's songs rang across the skies of Brazil. Now that blue vastness is silenced by his passing. And we who love him pray his extraordinary voice will soon be heard again.

CHAGDUD TULKU RINPOCHE

The Legacy of Pure Motivation

Rinpoche, you have lived and taught in many countries over the years. In your experience, what teachings are most important for all of us to hear?

OF ALL THE BUDDHIST TEACHINGS, PERHAPS NONE IS MORE IMPORTANT than that on pure motivation. If I were to leave only one legacy, it would be the wisdom of pure motivation. If I were to be known by one title, I would like it to be "motivation lama." Such motivation begins with compassion for the predicament of sentient beings. It culminates in the enlightened manifestation of spontaneous, uninterrupted benefit for those beings.

To establish the motivation of a bodhisattva, we begin by cultivating compassion, the powerful wish to alleviate suffering wherever it arises. The aspiration that sentient beings find happiness, both temporary and ultimate, adds the element of love. We recognize that all beings are equal in having been our mothers and are alike in their wish for happiness—no matter how misguided or frustrated their methods of obtaining it may be. This recognition serves as the starting point for equanimity. Vast equanimity arises with the realization that the essential nature of all beings is buddha nature; and although that nature goes unrecognized beneath layers of karmic obscurations and habitual patterns, beings' potential for enlightenment is never diminished, stained or lost. We can rejoice in this underlying buddha nature of beings, just as we can rejoice when their virtue brings them happiness. This is the source of spiritual joy.

The four qualities of compassion, love, equanimity and joy can manifest spontaneously from our buddha nature and suddenly motivate us to seek the spiritual path. Then, in a kind of upward spiral, when we hear, contemplate and meditate on the teachings about pure motivation, we are inspired to cultivate these four immeasurable qualities more deeply. At no point on the path of dharma do these qualities or the motivation to develop them become irrelevant. Rather, they begin to inform our every action of body, speech and mind. They are supported by vows: our refuge vow to refrain from harm, the bodhisattva vow to seek the enlightenment of all beings, and the Vajrayana vow to maintain nondual recognition of the essential purity of all phenomena.

In the moment that our heart moves toward compassion for all beings, our motivation expands toward the all-embracing motivation of a bodhisattva. Unable to bear the suffering of others, vowing to work constantly for the welfare of all, the bodhisattva seeks enlightenment in order to lead others to that same state. If we cultivate the bodhisattva's pure intention, then every

aspect of our spiritual practice, whether of purification or generating merit, takes on new meaning. By taming our own minds and accomplishing virtue, we can powerfully influence and benefit others. By following the superb examples of the bodhisattvas before us, we cut through self-clinging and freely offer to others whatever is positive. Our compassion matures and ultimately gives rise to unobscured, sky-like awareness.

Through the selfless motivation of a bodhisattva, we eventually accomplish the two benefits—compassionate manifestation for others and realization of mind's true nature for ourselves. That is why all Vajrayana sadhana practices open with preliminary prayers that establish our bodhisattva motivation. In the main practice, the deities, peaceful and wrathful alike, embody the qualities of compassion. Likewise, all sadhanas close with the sealing of pure motivation, when, through prayers of dedication, the merit of the practice is offered for the benefit of sentient beings. Thus, each stage of the sadhanas reestablishes great-minded motivation. Without this, practice is hollow, a mere pretense.

We read in the teachings that until all ignorance ends, the suffering of beings will continue. And for myself, it does seem that as soon as I have managed one painful situation, another is often upon me. How are we to develop great-minded motivation for others when we are inundated by such experiences?

Suffering is a powerful motivating force. By recognizing the cycles of our affliction, the depths of sorrow, we become inspired to uproot the cause by purifying our attachment and aversion and the endless array of mental obscurations and poisons that result from them. Suffering motivates us to learn what to accept and reject, to refine our conduct, to cultivate a connection to what is truly beneficial. Eventually, our deluded self-interest is transformed into the discerning self-interest of the spiritual practitioner who does not choose to be pulled, helplessly, repeatedly, into the undertow of samsaric suffering.

As our spiritual practice evolves, meditation enables us to cut through our attachment and aversion. We then experience the unfolding of our innate compassion, and our motivation begins to derive strength from altruistic concern for others' suffering. We are not the only ones in this ocean of samsara; countless others are sinking into dark depths beyond our seeing, beyond our imagination, in realms invisible to us, realms of unbearable pain.

If our mother were drowning or trapped in a burning house, would we not rush to help her? The teachings of Lord Buddha tell us that these countless beings are not distant strangers. All of them in some past lifetime have been our own kind mother who allowed us to take birth from her body, who protected our life, taught us and served our childhood needs. Now these past mothers have forgotten their relationship to us, and we likewise have forgotten their kindness. So we appear to each other as friends, enemies, strangers, colleagues and so on in an infinite spectrum of relationships. Ignorant of the past, we participate in the drama of the present and are oblivious, indifferent or even harmful toward each other.

My motivation is far from perfect. Though I strive to maintain pure intention,
self-interest seeps in everywhere.

It is naive to think that without guidance we can fully understand the Buddhist teachings or completely transform our self-centered motivation into the pure, transcendent intent of the buddhas and bodhisattvas. For this reason, we rely on the infallible wisdom and example of Buddha Shakyamuni; on his methods—the dharma; and on those who have an affinity for virtue and are motivated to practice the Buddha's teachings—the sangha. We seek out teachers accomplished in knowledge and meditation, and listen to their words. We ask questions if necessary, then contemplate and explore the meaning of the teachings until we have a genuine intellectual understanding. Finally, we meditate, seeking a direct experience that is beyond mere intellect.

When the steps of listening, contemplation and meditation are applied to the teachings on motivation, we learn its true meaning and how enlightened beings have exemplified it. Then we check our own motivation in everything we do, say or think. If we check carefully, we may find that the five poisons of ignorance, selfish attachment, anger, pride and jealousy taint even our virtuous activities. Recognizing such stains and purifying them is extremely important, because the outcomes of our actions correspond to our motivation. For example, two people might perform the same act of virtue, one with pure motivation, the other with motivation blemished by pride and competitiveness. The effects of the two acts will be different—the one performed with pure motivation will result in greater and more long lasting benefit.

We all want suffering to cease, Rinpoche, but the world is ravaged by it.
It is so painful to watch. How should we think about this?

The suffering of the six realms is limitless. Of the countless beings trapped in the endless cycles of samsaric rebirth, many experience a depth and duration of suffering that we cannot comprehend. We must not deny or turn away from this; and yet, as masters of meditation, holders of realization know, suffering is illusory, samsara is illusory—the whole display of relative reality is illusory. Nowhere can we find phenomena that are permanent, uncompounded and true. In our ordinary world, everything has come together, and everything will fall apart. Nothing lasts.

Our Lord Buddha told us that phenomena are like dreams, bubbles or optical illusions, like phantom cities, mirages, flickers of light or echoes. We ourselves are mere apparitions participating in a momentary, magical display even as our body, speech, thoughts and emotions constantly change and vanish.

At the moment of death, which represents our most dramatic confrontation with impermanence, we find ourselves stripped of everything, in a state of naked awareness that we may or may not recognize as the very nature of our mind. If we do not recognize it, the karmic forces that we have generated in countless lifetimes will propel us toward a new rebirth. Our cycling in samsara will never stop until we penetrate the illusion and recognize its unchanging, absolute nature.

But if everything is illusory, a dream, then one could think,
why bother to develop good qualities?

Right now, this illusion is our powerful and inescapable reality, and we haven't yet cut through our fixation on it. We can improve the illusion through virtuous conduct and the merit it generates. We can awaken from the illusion by hearing, contemplating and meditating on the wisdom teachings. But if we are careless and indifferent, we risk losing our precious spiritual opportunity and sinking deeper into obscuration, benefiting no one, neither others nor ourselves.

For this reason, we should return to the bodhisattva's motivation as our aspiration, as our measure of accomplishment, as our compass on the path. When we are tempted by worldly indulgence, we look at the example of the buddhas and bodhisattvas before us, at their tireless dedication to the welfare and liberation of sentient beings, their unflagging aspiration to reach enlightenment. We pray that our own pure motivation will only increase and become their all-encompassing compassion and wisdom. We invoke their blessings so that we may find ultimate realization.

When we are discouraged and beset with obstacles, we bring to mind the countless beings in samsara and think, "Oh, my sorrowful mothers, trapped in the web of samsaric delusion, if I have obstacles as a spiritual practitioner, how much greater are yours? If I abandon you, how will you ever find release? If I abandon my quest for enlightenment, how many of you will be bereft of a spiritual connection?" Then we pray that we will fully accomplish our training as a bodhisattva, benefiting beings constantly until the realms of samsara are empty. In this way, the teachings on motivation will unlock our hearts and minds now and guide us until we attain buddhahood. Then, the fulfillment of our enlightened intention will be spontaneous and never ending.

TULKU PEMA WANGYAL RINPOCHE

Meeting

TULKU PEMA WANGYAL RINPOCHE

DURING THE DUDJOM TERSAR INITIATIONS OF 1977 IN NEPAL, Tulku Pema Wangyal Rinpoche sometimes came to our house to visit Dungsey Thinley Norbu Rinpoche. Tulku Rinpoche was so extremely polite and soft-spoken that knowing what to say to him was always difficult. It seemed my voice would be incongruously loud in contrast to his gentleness, so I didn't try to converse. Usually I just bowed self-consciously and offered tea, attempting to mimic the grace of Tibetan manners.

Not long after meeting Tulku Rinpoche, it happened one day that I was very upset and crying. I left the house for privacy, walking up a deserted, dusty footpath between the rice paddies behind Boudha stupa. I was looking down in discouragement, and nearly collided with Rinpoche. It was a meeting that turned out to be very significant.

Because I was obviously distressed and he was extremely kind, Rinpoche stopped me and said quietly, "Please don't be so upset. Try to do this if you can: think about how many people right this minute have pain just as you do, how many are crying just as you are. Think about all the people everywhere who are having the same experience. Then call their pain into you. With every breath, take their grief into you. From deep inside your heart, breathe out comfort and compassion to those beings, soothing them and giving them everything they need. Try to keep doing this—it will help you." Having never heard this teaching, I was surprised by the words, yet calmed. I thanked Rinpoche and did as he advised. Sad to say, though, I rarely used those teachings until years later when a tragedy occurred on a remote and narrow Indian road.

During a journey to Guru Rinpoche's holy place of Tsopema—the only trip I took without my children—our bus was forced off a cliff by an oncoming vehicle and plummeted hundreds of feet into the ravine below. Though it is difficult to imagine, there were almost eighty people inside the bus and another forty balanced precariously on the roof. I was sitting on my suitcase in the rear and was swept out the back door as we tipped. Falling through the air, I saw the bus fly over me, and in that moment, saw a vision of my guru in the sky. I asked him in my mind, "Now what am I supposed to do? Look at this." He answered, "Pray to Guru Rinpoche," and so I began shouting, *"Om ah hung vajra guru padma siddhi hung,"* the mantra of Guru Rinpoche. I rolled myself into a ball as my mother had told me to do "if you ever fall," and eventually landed partway down the cliff on a small grassy ledge with some of the others. As we lay on the mountainside, the canyon echoed with the sound of the bus slamming against the walls of the ravine, the screams, and the voices of women calling for their children.

A boy, perhaps four years old, was lying next to me, his nose and mouth completely gone. Neither of us could move, but as he stared at me his eyes blinked slowly, showing he was still alive. Instinctively I began to do as Tulku Rinpoche had instructed years ago. I breathed in pain and thought of breathing out love to the boy and the others. Tulku Rinpoche's teachings pervaded everything during the hours of waiting, until I was carried up the mountain on a narrow board, and balanced in the backseat of a taxi for the twenty-hour ride to a small New Delhi hospital. Though I had thirteen fractures, there was relatively little pain for me during that long rescue. But only half of us survived the day.

I spent some months in the hospital. During recovery, the bright spot of the afternoons was watching the flock of peacocks that freely roamed the grounds, feasting on small mountains of garbage near the road. They brought to mind the first teaching I received from Kyabje Dudjom Rinpoche; he had said that all experience can be used to increase wisdom, just as peacocks can eat poison and become even more ravishing. And indeed, the peacocks outside my window did seem to become more lovely each day.

Tulku Rinpoche now stays primarily in France. Fulfilling the wishes of his father, Kangyur Rinpoche, he has established several retreat centers in the tranquil Dordogne region, where scores of western students study and practice. A great number of Nyingma masters have gone there to teach. All of this is supported by the kind vision of Tulku Pema Rinpoche.

When I visited Rinpoche in France to request the teaching that follows, I tried to express my gratitude to him for the words of wisdom he had spoken so many years ago. He looked puzzled, perhaps because the teaching of tonglen (taking in pain and giving out love) is very well known in the Mahayana tradition. But the impact of Rinpoche's compassion that day in Boudhanath and the power of this profound Buddhist teaching are unforgettable.

TULKU PEMA WANGYAL RINPOCHE

Looking into the Mirror of Our Present Life

IT IS NOT A SIMPLE THING TO TALK ABOUT A SPIRITUAL PATH, particularly about the teachings of the Buddha. One has to be well qualified. As for myself, being fortunate enough to have met some authentic and qualified Tibetan Buddhist teachers, I can simply repeat a few points I have heard from them. My first teacher, Kangyur Rinpoche, who also raised me, used to say that whatever we set out to do in life, we should always try to begin it with the thought of others. We should check our attitude. If it is positive and genuinely focused on benefiting others, then even if what we do is not perfect the results will be quite positive. Kyabje Dudjom Rinpoche and Kyabje Khyentse Rinpoche, as well as other great masters, would often say, "I am just one person; others are innumerable. Thinking of others is more important than thinking of myself."

In the vastness of space throughout the universe, and even on this earth, sentient beings are innumerable. But there is not a single one with whom we are not connected. As the great master Nagarjuna said, "From time immemorial in this universe, we are connected to one another in order to come into being." We are all dependent on each other, and when we come into existence through birth, we are particularly dependent on the kindness of our mother and father.

This is not our first life. We have come into this world many, many times. As Nagarjuna said, there is not a single being who has not been our parent, and there is not a single being we have not carried in our womb. Even if you search throughout the universe, you will never find a place even as small as the tip of a needle about which you can say, "This is a place where I was not born; this is a place where I did not die."

If you want to know how you have been in the past, simply look into the mirror of your present life. As the teachings say, this present life is the result of our past actions, and our future lives depend on our present actions. When we say "actions," we're including those of mind and speech, not just actions of the body. A happy and pleasant life is the reflection of positive actions. Whether we become a human, an animal or some other being, those forms of life manifest as a result of our past actions. Likewise, we are the creators of our future worlds, lives and perceptions. It is not possible to plant a rice seed and get an apple as a result.

How can we be sure we're planting the right seeds for our future lives?

We should start all our endeavors with the thought of others, particularly with the idea of bringing freedom from suffering and freedom from the causes of suffering to all sentient beings. We can call this a perfect beginning. At the time of acting, our mind should not perceive the things we do as concrete, nor should it cling to the subject of our actions. That is, we should not conceptualize or grasp at the subject, object or action. Then we can realize the perfect middle. Finally, we should complete whatever we have done by dedicating our merit so that all beings may achieve ultimate freedom from suffering and its causes. This is the perfect end.

Rinpoche, will you please speak more about mothers, who are referred to so often in the Buddhist scriptures? In some cultures today, we tend to hold mothers accountable for many of our present circumstances or psychological difficulties, so the term "mother love" may not have the resonance it once did.

In the teachings, there is an emphasis on mother sentient beings. Why is this emphasis so important even in these times, you ask? It is because of the selfless quality of a mother's love. These days, when we are traveling, if we ask someone to provide us with shelter for the night, the first thing we hear is "Where is your photo ID, your credit card?" Only if we have these things will we be given lodging in a hotel. If we can't produce them, it will be quite difficult to find a place to stay. By contrast, think about a future mother. A person unknown to her asks for shelter, not just in her house, but in her own body. She offers that shelter, not only for one day or a weekend, but for more than nine months.

In general, when even a small foreign object like a splinter enters our body, we immediately try to get rid of it. It is different for a mother. When a past karmic connection ripens and a mother conceives a child, in most cases a bond of love and honor develops between them. After the birth, there is nothing the mother considers more beautiful or precious than her infant. Even if the child is very demanding, still the mother will take care of the baby as best she can. We should remember: not only one sentient being but all sentient beings have been our mother in that same way, and not only once, but many, many, many times before. That is why it is important for us to think of all others as if they were our own loving mother.

The buddhas and bodhisattvas respond to all beings with this unconditional "mother love." Their hearts are completely soaked with true and genuine compassion. This is bodhicitta; this is the mind that is set on enlightenment. It is what enables them to take on the responsibility of benefiting others and allows them to progress along the path, ultimately achieving buddhahood.

Ordinary beings think only of themselves, and this is what keeps them wandering in the vicious circle of rebirth. Bodhicitta is most important for our progress on the spiritual path. It is a means of purifying our past negative actions and obscurations. We find examples of bodhicitta in the lives of all the great masters.

There is an ancient story of a meditation practitioner named Asanga, who began retreat so that he could have a vision of Maitreya Buddha and ask him for spiritual teachings. After spending three years in his meditation cave, he had no visions or signs of accomplishment, and he left in discouragement. On the way, he came across a man whose house was kept in perpetual shade by a tall rock. The man was trying to wear this rock away with a wet feather so that the sun would shine on his house. When Asanga saw this, he realized that he needed to develop more diligence in his practice, so he returned to his cave and continued to meditate on Maitreya.

After three more years, still having had no sign of achievement, he left again. This time, Asanga met someone trying to polish an iron rod into a needle using only a soft cloth. He realized then that he had still not been diligent enough and returned to his cave with renewed determination.

After three more long years of retreat without a sign, not even an auspicious dream, he left his retreat for the third time. On his journey, he stopped for the night in a small cave, where he heard a peculiar sound—"tick, tick, tick." Asanga saw a place where water was constantly dripping from above, gradually but surely making a hole in the rock below. He thought to himself, "If I persist in my efforts just a bit more, I might be able to achieve my goal." Again he returned to his retreat. But even after three more years of meditation, Asanga still had no sign of accomplishment and once again left his cave in discouragement.

This time, on the road he came across a bitch whose pitiful body was half rotten with wounds full of maggots. Feeling great compassion and love for the unfortunate creature, Asanga had the wish to remove the maggots from her wounds but at the same time did not want to kill them. So closing his eyes, he tried to remove them delicately with his tongue. But his tongue touched only the earth. When Asanga opened his eyes, the bitch had disappeared. In her place stood Lord Maitreya.

Asanga complained, "I have been meditating for the past twelve years without having had a single good dream or sign of you. Now, today, when I was simply trying to help this bitch, you finally appeared to me." Lord Maitreya said, "From the day you began your retreat, I was always with you, but your own obscurations prevented you from seeing me. Due to your twelve years of practice, you purified many of those stains. Today you have given birth to true compassion, which has completely purified your remaining obscurations. That is why you can see me now. If you do not believe what I say is true, then take me on your shoulder and walk through the bazaar asking others what they see."

Asanga set off happily with Maitreya balanced on his shoulder, wanting to show him to the world. But instead he found that most people said, "You must be crazy. Are you a lunatic? There's nothing on your shoulder." Only one very old woman whose obscurations were few said, "Oh, you are carrying a sick dog!" Lord Maitreya then took Asanga to Tushita Heaven and gave him many teachings, including the Five Teachings of Maitreya.

> *If we keep thinking of others, will that be enough for us to make*
> *progress on the path to enlightenment?*

A bird would have difficulty flying with just one wing, but with two wings will easily soar to its destination. In the same way, to achieve our goal of freeing others and ourselves, it is very important that the two wings of compassion and wisdom be present and balanced. When we say, "I wish to achieve buddhahood for the sake of others," that wish for buddhahood is wisdom, while intending to attain it for the sake of others is compassion. It is important to combine the two. Without compassion, knowledge will be merely intellectual. Without wisdom, compassion will be very emotional and will not help us transcend samsara, cyclic existence.

Wisdom helps us to transcend samsara. Compassion helps us to transcend another limit or extreme, that of a static nirvana. It was through the realization of compassionate wisdom that the Buddha succeeded in going beyond samsara and nirvana. This might sound very abstract, but actually it is something we can apply every day. For example, when giving even a mouthful of food to an animal or to a person in need, we should simply give it without emotion, without expecting anything in return. That is the wisdom aspect. At the same time, if we maintain the wish to help others as a mother would take care of her only child, that is the compassion aspect. We will have far fewer obstacles in fulfilling our own goals if we keep such an attitude. His Holiness the Dalai Lama says in his teachings that the more we say "me, me, me," thinking only of ourselves, the more problems we will have. But the more we think of others, the fewer and lighter our troubles will be. In our daily lives, if we really want peace and happiness for others and ourselves, the most important thing for us to cultivate is this unconditional love and compassion. Let us take this to heart.

ORGYEN TOPGYAL RINPOCHE

M Y FIRST INTRODUCTION TO THE GREAT ORGYEN TOPGYAL RINPOCHE simply consisted of watching him from afar. Even from a distance, his charismatic and imposing figure stood out. Rinpoche was assisting Kyabje Dilgo Khyentse Rinpoche during the 1978 Chokling Tersar initiations in Nepal, which were attended by thousands of people.

As one of Dilgo Khyentse Rinpoche's close students, Orgyen Topgyal Rinpoche often led the most forceful and potent dharmapala ceremonies performed in a separate shrine room within the monastery. I would sometimes watch from the doorway during these pujas just to be in proximity to him and the fiercely compelling sound of steady drumbeats and chants. In my perception, Rinpoche exuded a relaxation born of complete concentration, and it was hard to imagine a more precise and masterful guardian of the Buddhadharma. In those days—some twenty years ago—I assumed that Rinpoche was "wrathful," perhaps because of the juxtaposition of his often serious countenance and the strong physical stature lent by his Khampa blood. This assumption was far from true, however.

It wasn't until years later, when Rinpoche gave teachings at our home in California, that I had the honor of spending some time with him. He spoke and acted in a very direct, concise manner, accomplishing what needed to be done without wasted words, time or movement. As focused as he was when teaching, Rinpoche seemed equally carefree and funny during his moments of relaxation.

Five years after Rinpoche's visit, I went to northern India to visit his monastery in the village of Bir and request that he give a teaching. Unfortunately, he had just left unexpectedly for Hong Kong. One of his monks took pity on me and offered a guided tour of the monastery compound. Most memorable was the newly created Guru Rinpoche statue housed in the prayer hall. The spectacular image fills the room, reaching nearly to the top of the very high ceiling. The face has been painted with a fine and delicate hand and gives the impression that the great Guru's eyes are trained on you wherever you sit. Seated there, I felt as though the room was pervaded by the Guru's presence, awakening memories of the teachings that had kindled my devotion to the Buddhadharma.

After returning to the United States, I telephoned Rinpoche, who was by now in Colorado. Since he wasn't going to be there long, he told me to come the next day. The teaching that follows here was then given in Boulder, where the venerable Trungpa Rinpoche established one of the first Vajrayana Buddhist communities in North America. This small college town continues to be a magnet for Buddhist teachers and students, and on the way to meet Rinpoche, I saw several houses flying colorful Tibetan prayer flags. It was a wonderful morning; the flow of Orgyen Topgyal Rinpoche's voice expounding the Buddhadharma is like the inevitable flow of a confident river. Sitting in his commanding and magnetic presence was like being cloaked in the undiluted Nyingma Buddhist teachings.

ORGYEN TOPGYAL RINPOCHE

The Unerring Path in the Nyingma Tradition
and the Importance of Prayer

THE UNERRING PATH THAT ENSURES BENEFIT AND HAPPINESS for all beings, in the short and long term, is the practice of the dharma taught by the perfectly enlightened Buddha.

Rinpoche, would you please give an explanation of some of the skillful methods that are used in Vajrayana Buddhism, particularly those unique to the Nyingma tradition?

In the practice of the dharma there are different approaches, or yanas—two, three, even nine can be discussed. The quintessential and consummate level of these approaches is found in the Great Perfection (Dzogchen) teachings. Those who practice the Great Perfection follow the early translation school, or Nyingma school.

When Buddhism first flourished in the holy country of India, there was no distinction between Nyingma and Sarma, which are the newer schools. It was after the teachings came to Tibet that this distinction arose, and the oldest of the spiritual traditions in Tibet became known as the Nyingma, or Ancient School. Who gave it this name? It was those who followed the newer schools, known collectively as the Sarma. Their statement, "You Nyingma are the eldest," was based on their appreciation of the Nyingma having the excellent, most profound and most complete teachings. "We," they said, "represent an innovation." To use an English expression, the Sarmas considered theirs to be a more modern spiritual tradition. But if you really think about it, the older a spiritual tradition is, the more substantial it is. The farther we can trace a tradition back, the closer its roots are to the time of our Teacher—the Buddha, the Blessed One—the better. This is Nyingma.

As for the ways in which the Nyingma teachings are transmitted and practiced, there are three major lines of transmission: extensive transmission, or kama, from Vajradhara Buddha to your own root guru; more direct transmission, or terma; and profound visionary transmission, or daknang. In all of these, it is said that the actual practice consists of meditating on the stage of development, meditating on the stage of completion, and then integrating these two stages. This profound path of integrating the stages of development and completion is termed "sadhana," or "means of accomplishment." There are sadhanas associated with all of the Three Roots: the gurus as the root of blessing; the chosen deities, or yidams, as the root of spiritual attainment; and the dakinis and dharmapalas as the root of enlightened activity. Although thousands, even

millions of such sadhanas have been taught, these all condense to a means of attainment that focuses on the guru, or "guru sadhana."

Of all these guru sadhanas, the ones that are held to be most sacred are those that focus on Guru Rinpoche as the union of the Three Roots. Guru Rinpoche himself said:

> To accomplish my state is to accomplish that of all buddhas;
> To behold me is to behold all buddhas.

Some of the sadhanas focusing on Guru Rinpoche as the chosen deity are associated with the Eight Commands, or Kagye. The Eight Commands were transmitted to Guru Rinpoche by masters of awareness who had realized the sublime state of Mahamudra. These practices unite Guru Rinpoche with a chosen deity. For example, in certain practices called "Lapur Drakma" (combination of Guru and Kila), Guru Rinpoche is the guru aspect and Vajrakilaya is the deity aspect. There are similar practices uniting Guru Rinpoche with Yamantaka or Guru Rinpoche with Hayagriva. All such deity-oriented practices derive from the vast ocean of collected teachings that Guru Rinpoche transmitted; their root also lies in the sadhana of Guru Rinpoche. A sadhana of Guru Rinpoche can be oriented from the point of view of the guru principle or that of the chosen deities or that of the dakinis, because while the outer level of practice focuses on Guru Rinpoche, his inner body mandala includes the deities of the Eight Commands, the dakinis and the dharmapalas. Such sadhanas include the "Tsasum Gongdü" (Union of the Enlightened Intent of the Three Roots).

Would you please also speak about the use of prayer in sadhana practice?

Sadhanas are means of accomplishment that rely on the use of mantra. Mantra is not merely words repeated over and over; mantras are a form of prayer. From this point of view, the mantra *Om ah hung vajra guru padma siddhi hung* is a prayer to invoke Guru Rinpoche. The foundation of sadhana, then, lies in prayer. When you practice, do it with a sense of surrender, focusing on Guru Rinpoche as inseparable from your own root guru and trusting in him as an infallible source of refuge. This source of refuge embodies the union of the Three Jewels; the union of the Three Roots; the union of the channels, subtle energies and bindu; and the union of the three kayas—dharmakaya, the empty essence of mind; sambhogakaya, its lucid nature; and nirmanakaya, its distinct manifestations. If you understand this all to be the display of mind, and pray to your root guru as inseparable from Guru Rinpoche, this form of practice is beyond compare. Therefore, prayer is always extremely important.

If you do not understand how to pray to your guru with conviction and devotion, no matter how many millions of mantras you recite, no matter how much you meditate on any number of peaceful and wrathful deities, no matter how much you examine your mind in the stage of completion, this all amounts to tiring yourself for no purpose. On the other hand, if you pray to your guru with devotion, blending your mind with the guru's enlightened mind, then even if you are not reciting prayers aloud, you are praying from the depths of your heart with a sense of trust and conviction. To pray in this way to Guru Rinpoche, inseparable from your own guru, is the way the real merit of prayer is found. It brings unfailing benefit in this lifetime, in the intermediate state after death, and in future lifetimes. That is why prayer is so important. By praying, one can gain sublime and more ordinary spiritual attainments effortlessly and spontaneously in a single lifetime.

With respect to prayer, people may wonder, "Should we use the Seven-Line Prayer? Should we recite Calling the Lama from Afar?" Of course it is good to recite such prayers; for instance, the Seven-Line Prayer is the quintessence of all the terma teachings of the Nyingma school. But again it is not crucial that you recite prayers aloud; what is crucial is to feel a sense of trust and conviction from the depths of your heart. Such prayer is most important.

Given the importance of prayer, if you pray in this way, all the principles of sadhana practice are complete. All the effects of practicing the stages of development and completion come about through prayer. In the practice of Dzogchen, prayer to your guru invokes the grace and blessing that ensure your realization of the Great Perfection. Prayer brings about the experiences of the trekchö path of original purity or the visions of tögal, the path of spontaneous presence, so that you reach a consummate level of accomplishment. Finally, in the expanse where all phenomena resolve into their true nature, you will awaken to buddhahood.

SOGYAL RINPOCHE

Meeting
SOGYAL RINPOCHE

WHEN KYABJE DUDJOM RINPOCHE CAME TO THE UNITED STATES IN 1976, Sogyal Rinpoche was his first translator. Rinpoche had studied at Cambridge University, so he spoke in articulate English, brushed with a faint British accent. He had an uncanny ability not only to convey Dudjom Rinpoche's words but also to inspire. He himself would give explanatory teachings on the weekends. Listening to Sogyal Rinpoche speak about the great gurus aroused one's own best nature; lingering complacency was replaced by a piercing devotion.

After we moved to Nepal, I would see Sogyal Rinpoche only occasionally when he visited Kathmandu to attend initiations and ceremonies. When we moved back to the United States from France in 1985, however, I was to meet him more often. We hadn't lived American lives in more than nine years, so returning to the West was a bit of a shock. It was Sogyal Rinpoche and his students who eased the transition. We settled in the town of Aptos, where Rinpoche has a home overlooking the California coast, and I would see him there when he visited the United States. Rinpoche's students would converge on the house during those times, drawn not just by Rinpoche's motivating teachings but also by the atmosphere of joy and abundance he creates wherever he goes.

Rinpoche's generosity toward everyone around him was remarkable and manifested in both mundane and extraordinary ways. He was constantly giving; there seemed to be an endless supply of small gifts. Pictures of Guru Rinpoche, Tibetan calendars and small statues were pressed into the hands of visitors as they left. Rinpoche struck me as some sort of magician who couldn't help but pull treasures out of his sleeve. Most of all, Rinpoche gave to others by bringing great masters to the West, wanting everyone to have the opportunity to meet Dudjom Rinpoche, Khyentse Rinpoche, the Dalai Lama, Nyoshul Khenpo Rinpoche and many others.

Rinpoche's teachings were a constant stream of praise to the great Buddhist masters and saints. He often spoke of his own master, Jamyang Khyentse Chökyi Lodrö, who had helped raise him. He would tell us that when one walked into the presence of this great guru, one would notice that the sweet fragrance from his body scented the entire house as if with perfume. Listening to Sogyal Rinpoche reminisce afforded dharma students a rare vision of old Tibet.

In the spring of 2003, I called Rinpoche's assistant to request a meeting with him about this book, and he told me we could meet in France. In August, my daughter and I arrived in Paris on the hottest day in the city's history. The asphalt was liquid with heat as we drove south to Montpellier and then to the higher terrain of Rinpoche's center, Lerab Ling. Parched meadows lined the road for much of the journey, but as we climbed, the air grew cool and the pastures green. As we turned the final bend of the winding road, a patch of pine trees came into view at the top of a hill, their tall forms anchoring streams of prayer flags, colors winking in the breeze.

The trees shaded a tall, red arch stretching over the entrance to a small gravel road. Signs were posted requesting silence, and we walked quietly down the path. On one side was an expansive meadow where small chalets were lined up in tidy rows, their doors facing the main shrine tent. As we came closer, we heard the deep rumble of chanting coming from several loudspeakers. Approaching the main tent, we saw Sogyal Rinpoche seated on a riser surrounded by several hundred people. It was Guru Rinpoche's birthday—a very auspicious occasion—and Rinpoche was leading his students in a traditional feast offering, or tsok.

We joined the tsok practice, which had been in progress since dawn. Before the dinner break, Rinpoche told the group to prepare for a long night; we would be reciting a hundred thousand tsok offering prayers before sleep. All three hundred participants kept track of their prayers, and the practice was completed at 3:30 in the morning. Rinpoche's energy never lagged. The night was punctuated by occasional breaks during which he played taped teachings and chanting by Dudjom Rinpoche, Khyentse Rinpoche or Chagdud Rinpoche. The upwelling of devotion in the room was palpable, and it felt as though these masters were actually there with us.

The next day, when we returned for an interview with Rinpoche, he agreed to give a teaching on the subject of death and dying, a topic for which he has become well known. I took photos of Rinpoche in his new garden, a waterfall trickling behind him. Rinpoche was as generous as ever, allowing a visit to the shrine room in his home where so many great lamas had stayed, and when we departed, it was with gifts of pictures and books in our hands.

SOGYAL RINPOCHE

In the Mirror of Death

Thank you for this opportunity, Rinpoche.
Could you please give us some guidance on impermanence and death, in particular
on how we can relate to the process of dying in a more natural way?

"Learn to die and thou shalt learn how to live. There shall none learn how to live that hath not learned to die." These words, written hundreds of years ago in the medieval *Book of the Craft of Dying,* often come into my mind when I think about our understanding of death and its relationship to life. If we can only learn how to face death, then we will have learned the most important lesson of life: how to face ourselves, and thus come to terms with ourselves in the deepest possible sense, as human beings.

In this modern age, we do not look at life and death as a whole. As a result, we become very attached to this life, and we reject and deny death. Death becomes our ultimate fear, the very last thing we want to look at. I often tell people, if you're concerned about dying, don't worry; we will all die, quite successfully. Then why are we so afraid of death? Beneath our fear of death is a fear of looking into and facing ourselves, because the moment of death is the moment of truth. In fact, death is like a mirror in which the true meaning of life is reflected.

Unfortunately, in modern life people look at death as a kind of loss or as a defeat. However, from a spiritual point of view, death is not a tragedy to be feared, but an opportunity for transformation. Death is our greatest teacher. It wakes us up so that we don't become slothful, lazy or naive. The trouble with us is that even though we know we will die one day, because we do not know when or how it will happen, we think we have an unlimited lease on life, so we procrastinate.

I remember talking about this with one of my own masters, Dilgo Khyentse Rinpoche, one of the greatest masters of recent times and a teacher of His Holiness the Dalai Lama. He came to the West on a number of occasions during the latter part of his life, and on one of those visits, I asked him what he particularly noticed about people in the West. He replied, "Well, they have a tremendous interest in the teachings, but they waste so much time." I was surprised and asked him, "How can you say they waste time? They are always so busy." He told me that it was precisely because we are always so busy that we waste time, which causes us to forget the most important thing—death—and life for that matter.

Laziness has many different forms. In the modern world, the one most practiced is "active laziness." We keep ourselves so busy that we don't have time to think about and take care of the most important things. And so we fool ourselves. As it is said, "The mind is ingenious in the games of deception."

Death, on the other hand, tells us it's time to stop kidding ourselves. Coming to terms with death, then, is actually coming to terms with life. Yet all too often, it seems, we only start to think about death just before we die. But isn't that a bit too late? The teachings show us that we should prepare for death now, when we're well and in a happy frame of mind. It is particularly in those moments when we are naturally moved to introspection that we begin to see life and death in a more inspired and profound way.

As we reflect on death, we come to realize that we could die at any moment. So we have to be ready. After all, dying is actually very simple: you breathe out, and when you can't breathe in— that's it! Very simple, and very immediate.

Death is in every moment of our life. Living with the immediacy of death, or coming face to face with death, helps us to purify and simplify our lives and sort out our priorities. Isn't the "life review" at the moment of death—spoken of in many religions, as well as by those who have experienced "near death"—leaving it a bit too late? Essentially, then, what the teachings tell us is that by reflecting on death and impermanence, we can prepare for death now, in life.

As we reflect on life, we come to realize that everything in life is impermanent. Usually, we plan our lives, organize and arrange everything, and keep things as safe and secure as possible. Yet our security gets blown away when impermanence takes place—often in an unexpected way. Then we have no idea how to cope because we have not planned for it. So, if we wish to have a secure plan for life, we need to prepare on a deeper level and find an inner refuge. When you have that inner refuge, even though everything around you falls apart, there is something inside you that never gives up on you and never lets you down. That is what the teachings provide.

I often ask myself, "Why is everything impermanent? Why do things always change?" And only one answer ever comes back to me: "That is how life is." Life is impermanent; the discontinuity is a part of the fundamental continuity. For example, if a watch doesn't tick—move, change—it's not working, it's dead. If your heart is not beating, constantly changing, you are dead.

It is change that keeps life alive and provides us with the opportunity to change. Most of all, what impermanence teaches us is to let go of grasping, yearning and attachment, which only bring pain and suffering. The reason we become so fiercely attached to things—from our emotions, ideas and opinions to our possessions and other people—is that we have not taken impermanence to heart. Once we can accept that impermanence is the very nature of life and that everyone suffers, including ourselves, at the hands of change and death, then letting go becomes the only natural thing to do—in fact, the only thing that works. Then, our attachment to our grief is loosened and impermanence becomes a consolation, bringing us peace, confidence and fearlessness. And most important of all, we can see clearly how futile it is to grasp at something that is simply ungraspable.

Though we know that everything is by nature impermanent, somehow we can't accept it. Instead, we try to cheat this natural process, which is impossible because that goes against the very laws of nature. As a result, we get hurt. So all we have to do is accept impermanence once and for all. The extraordinary thing is that when you do accept death and impermanence, you realize you're not losing anything at all. In fact, you are gaining everything. It's as if you are losing the clouds but gaining the sky.

Rinpoche, could you speak about the moment of death?

From a spiritual point of view, the moment of death is considered to be the most important moment of our life. The fundamental message of the Buddhist teachings is that if we are prepared, there is tremendous hope, both in life and in death. For someone who has prepared and practiced, death comes not as a defeat but as a triumph, the crowning and most glorious moment of life. The moment of death is a tremendous opportunity if we understand clearly what is happening and we have prepared well for it in life. For at the actual moment of death, the thinking ego-mind dies into the essence. And in this truth, enlightenment takes place. If we familiarize ourselves with the true nature of mind through practice while we are still alive, then we become more prepared for it when it reveals itself spontaneously at the moment of death. Recognition then follows as naturally as a child running into its mother's lap. Remaining in that state, we are liberated.

What the teachings reveal is the wonderful "good news" that when this body dies, the ordinary mind and all its delusions die. All the thoughts and emotions related to anger, desire and ignorance die. What is revealed at the moment of death is the ultimate ground of our being, the buddha nature—the nature of our mind, sometimes called the Ground Luminosity or Clear Light. For a Christian practitioner, you could almost call this going back to God, as it is going back to our primordial nature. This essential nature of mind is the background to the whole of life and death, like the sky, which enfolds the whole universe in its embrace.

At the moment of death, there are two things that count: whatever we have done in our lives and what state of mind we are in at that moment. Even if we have accumulated a lot of harmful actions in our lives, if we are really able to make a change of heart at the moment of death, it can decisively influence our future and transform our karma, because the moment of death is an exceptionally powerful opportunity for purifying karma. If we die in a positive frame of mind, we can improve our next birth. This means that the last thought and emotion that we have before we die has an extremely powerful determining effect on our immediate future.

This is why the masters stress that the quality of the atmosphere around us when we die is crucial. With our friends and relatives, we should do all we can to inspire positive emotions and sacred feelings, like love, compassion and devotion, and do all that we can to help them let go of grasping, yearning and attachment.

How should we practice at the time of death, Rinpoche?

The great master Padmasambhava, founder of Tibetan Buddhism and revealer of *The Tibetan Book of the Dead,* gave the following advice for the moment of death:

> Now when the bardo of dying dawns upon me,
> I will abandon all grasping, yearning and attachment,
> Enter undistracted into clear awareness of the teaching,
> And eject my consciousness into the space of unborn Rigpa;
> As I leave this compound body of flesh and blood
> I will know it to be a transitory illusion.

Or more simply:

> Let go of attachment and aversion.
> Keep your heart and mind pure;
> Unite your mind with the wisdom mind of the buddhas;
> Rest in the nature of mind.

Rinpoche, how can we help someone who is dying to do as Padmasambhava said and abandon grasping, yearning and attachment?

You'll do it through the emotional care and support that you give the dying person, and the presence and love that you give them, which is inspired by your practice. If we have come in touch with the nature of our mind, stabilized it through our spiritual practice, and integrated it into our lives, then the love we have to give can only be deeper, because it comes from a deeper source: from our innermost being, the heart of our enlightened nature. It has a special power to free us or the dying person.

This kind of love, beyond all attachment, is like divine love. It is the love of all the buddhas, the love of Christ, the love of God. In that state, without contriving and even without thinking, we can feel the presence of the Buddha or of Christ, effortlessly. It's as if we become their ambassador, their representative, our love backed by their love and infused with their blessing and compassion. Love that springs truly from the nature of the mind is so blessed that it has the power to dispel the fear of the unknown, to give refuge from anxiety, to grant serenity and peace, and to bring inspiration in death and beyond. That is how you can help the dying person to "abandon grasping, yearning and attachment."

Secondly, Padmasambhava says, "Enter undistracted into the clear awareness of the teachings." If you're an accomplished practitioner, this is where you rest in the nature of mind. As we saw earlier, the culmination of your meditation training is to arrive at the essential nature of mind and to be able to rest in that state of Clear Light. And as was said earlier, when this body dies, the ordinary mind and all its delusions die; all the thoughts and emotions related to anger, desire and ignorance die, and the nature of the mind—the Clear Light—is revealed.

Now, you let go of all attachment and aversion and remain in meditation, in the clear awareness of the teaching which your master has introduced to you and which you have recognized and integrated through practice. At the moment of death, you can enter into that Clear Light of the nature of mind, and liberation is assured.

Or, if you have not fully realized the ultimate nature of mind, then you simply remember the most important point of the teachings. Go over all the teachings again and again. Gather their essence, and through practice, let it become the very heart and core and body of your understanding, so that it becomes "the clear awareness of the teachings." Then when you die, you can die with that awareness in your heart. This is what is really meant by "conscious dying."

Thirdly, Padmasambhava says, "And eject my consciousness into the space of unborn Rigpa." This is the practice of Phowa. In Tibet, when someone dies, to have a lama present is considered to be equally as important as having a doctor there. If possible, the family or friends of the dying person will bring several lamas, one after another, each to do a Phowa practice—but only those who have been properly trained. To do the traditional practice of Phowa you require very specific training; otherwise it may not be effected.

However, the practice that I've shared in *The Tibetan Book of Living and Dying,* called the Essential Phowa, can be practiced by anyone. It lies at the heart of the Tibetan Buddhist tradition and is not only the practice for the moment of death, but is also the most important practice in life and a powerful practice for healing. Traditionally it is called Lama'i Naljor in Tibetan or Guru Yoga in Sanskrit. Phowa practice is an aspect of Guru Yoga, and whatever your religion or spiritual tradition, it is possible to adapt it to your own faith. It is a practice you can do for yourself, and you can also do it for others.

The kind of death we have is so crucial; death is the most important moment of our lives, and all of us should be able to die with dignity, and in peace. I hope that in the years to come we can see a continuing revolution in the way we approach death and dying, one which carries the deepest spiritual values at its heart and which will give birth to different environments and places where people at all stages of living and dying can come to derive benefit.

NAMKHA DRIMED RINPOCHE

In the wake of the Communist invasion, it was India that opened her doors to Tibetans forced to leave much more than their mountains behind. For Namkha Drimed Rinpoche and his followers, the crossing took more than two years by foot and was aided by many brave Tibetan families along the way. Their journey ended in the eastern state of Orissa. It was there, in a hastily established refugee settlement, that Rinpoche and many Nyingma lamas made their new home and where his reputation as a terton began to grow.

When I took my two children to meet Namkha Drimed Rinpoche in 1979, the Orissa refugee camp had only begun the transformation into the stable community it is today, and there was much poverty. Things have changed greatly since then. Now, the residents drink clean water from the tap rather than from a drying, stagnant well. Many of the temporary shelters have been replaced by tidy houses. Instead of spending their days running barefoot on the cracked earth, the children learn to read in the local schoolhouse or join the monastery to train in Buddhist studies. It is no longer merely a refugee camp but a growing community of Tibetans practicing and educating others in Buddhist practice, art, dance and philosophy. Rinpoche now has a home and monastery in Nepal and visits the United States regularly. What remains unchanged is Namkha Rinpoche's ability to help others walk out of obstacles.

Some years ago when in Nepal, I was notified that a loved one was suffering from a serious health problem. Rinpoche was about to leave for Taiwan, so I raced frantically to the departure gate at the airport to request a divination and advice. He said that to ease this difficulty, he would have to come to my home in California and perform special ceremonies, but told me not to worry, because he would soon be in America. I returned to California, and as he had promised, when Rinpoche came to the United States, he made a detour to our house. During his stay, he performed those ceremonies, and for many days our quiet, conservative neighborhood by the sea enjoyed the unfamiliar sounds of old Tibet.

In the Nyingma tradition, when certain ceremonies are performed, there are certain things that go along with them. In part, the rituals involve musical offerings to the divine, one of the ways to transform ordinary phenomena into wisdom phenomena. And so every day, there were eight monks in the house with Rinpoche, playing thigh-bone trumpets—a unique, piercing sound; rhythmically pounding drums and ringing bells; offering three-foot-high tormas in the backyard or smuggling them out to be offered in the ocean; burning so much sandalwood and myrrh the entire street and surrounding golf course were perfumed. The neighbors would knock on the door—loudly, to be heard over the chanting—to ask what was going on and how much longer it would last. Thinking it would be difficult for them to understand "ceremony to expel negativity" and fearing they might call the local authorities, I said it was a Buddhist funeral ceremony. Sometimes, glancing out the window, I would see five or more of my neighbors lined up in the street below, staring up at our house on the hill in resigned shock. Every few days, one would venture nervously to the door and ask, "How much longer is your funeral going to go on?"

The ceremonies performed by Namkha Drimed Rinpoche helped immensely, and I am particularly grateful for the compassion that brought him to our home. The kindness of Rinpoche and the kindness of the Buddhadharma are unending.

NAMKHA DRIMED RINPOCHE

Understanding Relationships

Rinpoche, when I visited your family in Nepal and India, everyone seemed extraordinarily happy and harmonious. But here, these days, many of us find our family and work relationships wrought with problems which demand much of our time and energy. How can we better integrate spiritual practice and family life?

HAVING A FAMILY NEED NOT PREVENT YOU IN ANY WAY FROM PRACTICING DHARMA and attaining realization. Several generations ago in Tibet, my own great-grandfather, Shakya Shri, maintained a family, and his meditation practice was not disturbed in any way. Because of his practice, he attained realization and ultimately enlightenment. Spiritual practice does not require completely abandoning ordinary life and adopting the robes of a nun or monk. In Tibet, lamas sometimes alternate between conducting solitary retreat in a remote location and spending time with their families at home. In the West, you can follow their example by going on a short retreat and then returning home again to lead your day-to-day life.

When we speak about how to get along in our relationships, it's important to have some understanding of karma. In many Eastern countries, people believe there are numerous lifetimes and take this into consideration when making decisions. It seems more common in the West, however, to believe that we live just this one life. Lord Buddha taught about previous lifetimes and karma, and since I am a Buddhist lama, I am definitely going to speak about this!

For now let's consider two types of relationship. One is a karmic relationship and the other is more ordinary, you might say casual. In a casual relationship, a man and a woman come together for a short time simply out of desire. There is nothing special about that. No potent karma is involved, and they will drift apart when the desire is exhausted. However, meeting someone with whom you have a strong karmic connection from past lives is quite a different thing. The karmic link is already established, so there is greater potential for creating further karma. Not only that, individuals can establish patterns leading to similar relationships in future lives. When a man and woman come together and decide to become husband and wife, it is due to their very strong karmic connection, so the relationship must be handled carefully from the start.

How should we go about that?

It is important to keep some balance in your relationships. I've noticed that in the West many couples initially have an excessive attachment to each other, which can lead to strong aversion later on.

In the beginning, a couple is almost inseparable. They sit together, they stand together, they walk together and they sleep together. In fact, they do everything together, keeping their egos and negativity concealed. Then after a while, because they have done too much together in a very short time, they grow tired of one another. Neither is willing to tolerate the other. By this time, they may have financial problems and one or two children. Suddenly, they don't want to be married anymore.

People who have a slight understanding of dharma use karma as an excuse for a divorce, saying, "Oh, our karma has ended." Their karma has not ended; they have just changed their minds.

To have a fruitful and enduring marriage, it is important to build a stable foundation. In the long term, the couple should care for one another, always remembering that their union is due to a karmic connection. Each of them should think, "Whether times are good or bad, I will try to make my loved one happy." Each should also learn to compromise. By going in completely different directions, they can destroy their relationship. If a couple becomes just two people living in the same home but pursuing their individual interests without regard for each other, then generally they won't stay together.

Keep in mind it is not possible to have perfection all the time, and maintain tolerance and compassion toward your partner. No one can run away from suffering; suffering is inevitable. Try to be patient and endure—stormy emotions will pass. Even if the passion is gone, it is important to continue caring for one another. Remembering that you have come together because of a strong karmic connection, consider your future karma and try to withstand difficulties, particularly if you have children. If you leave each other prematurely, you can suffer tremendously because of all the negative karmic results. On the other hand, if you practice endurance, things will improve in the long run.

Rinpoche, you have told me that endurance is a profound way to purify karma,
and your words have encouraged me during prolonged difficult circumstances.
Please, will you speak further about endurance?

Yes. We can use anger as an example, since it is the most destructive of the ten nonvirtuous actions. When someone is angry with us and tries to start an argument, if we do not practice endurance in the situation, our own anger will arise and the fighting will escalate. The ego can become so involved that we cause severe harm to someone and, thinking we are victorious, even take joy in the other's pain. This creates the worst negative karma. However, if we can endure and feel compassion, the other person's anger will automatically subside and dissolve. Thus, the aggressor will not be accumulating any more nonvirtue. Since we have transformed the hostile emotions and aroused our own compassion, we ourselves will create virtue. Can you see why the practice of endurance is so profound?

You don't have to be Buddhist to do this. Everyone can practice endurance, and those who do so will benefit themselves and others. Actually, there is nothing better than endurance—it is an invaluable aspect of the spiritual path.

Rinpoche, I remember your saying that it took two years for you and thirty others to walk out of Tibet. That seems beyond endurance. You also told me that you guided the way using arrow divinations to choose which mountain passes were safe and when to travel. Actually I've heard many accounts of how your accurate divinations have helped others. Will you please speak some about this form of prophecy?

In Tibet during the time of King Gesar, arrow divinations were often performed. King Gesar himself had no need for such methods because he always had clear vision and prophecies came to him directly from Guru Rinpoche. However, Gesar's father and his thirty generals used this form of divination. I myself started using these divinations in 1956 and did rely on them as we walked across the mountains of Tibet and into India.

Performing the divination is an actual Gesar of Ling practice. To begin the divination, I meditate and recite a specific mantra. After the recitation, I blow on the arrows and ask the question. Two arrows are used. One, held in the right hand and covered with a white cloth, is the arrow of the gods. The other, held in the left hand and covered with a black cloth, is referred to as the demons' arrow. When you watch the arrows during the divination, you will observe that they move in different ways. You might think that I am moving them myself, but actually they move on their own. Whether the movement is forceful and swift or gentle and slow is not determined by me. This movement is interpreted according to the practice of Ling Gesar and is what determines the prophecy.

Thank you, Rinpoche. Before we finish, would you give a concise explanation of how virtuous actions create merit?

Yes, merit is good karma. It is a collection of our good deeds gathered together, forming a sort of "treasure." We carry this treasure in our mindstreams when we pass from this life. Even though we might enjoy fortunate circumstances now due to our past accumulation of merit, we must continue developing a virtuous mind in order to keep our treasury of merit full. Having greater concern for others, helping poor people, caring for the aged or doing something to better the world are some ways of accumulating merit. This brings us immense benefit in this and future lives.

Lord Buddha taught that we must care for all beings and not just ourselves. Please keep his words in your heart.

DZIGAR KONGTRUL RINPOCHE

Meeting
DZIGAR KONGTRUL RINPOCHE

IN 1977 THE GREAT BOUDHANATH STUPA was surrounded by terraced, jade rice paddies studded with the gold and white of Tibetan Buddhist monasteries. Often in the early mornings, we would wake to the sound of conch shells being blown, calling the monks to puja. Many tulkus studied here in their youth, with Kyabje Khyentse Rinpoche, Kyabje Dudjom Rinpoche and other great masters. In rare free moments, some of the young tulkus could be found surreptitiously reading Tintin comic books. My son shared their passion for Tintin, and so it happened that his large collection soon became Boudha's informal comic book library—for monks and tulkus only, he sternly insisted. That is how I was introduced to Dzigar Kongtrul Rinpoche. He was my favorite of the young tulkus I met there. Even though he was a teenager, a very important, distinguished tulku and a busy student, he would stop to converse with me, even in the streets of Kathmandu, and it always felt as though he was genuinely interested in my small world of family and study.

Remembering his steady kindness, I very much hoped Rinpoche would be a part of this book, even though we hadn't met in many years. It should have been easy to reestablish contact with Rinpoche. In response to his students' needs, he gives a dharma talk called "Personal Link" every Sunday morning via telephone conference call, which is open to anyone who would like to listen. Although his voice entered my home and he taught in person throughout the United States, still, by some strange confluence of circumstances, Dzigar Kongtrul Rinpoche proved to be one of the most difficult masters to locate.

I would repeatedly call his home in Colorado and find that he was in retreat or on his way to see students in faraway countries—Nepal, Japan, France; once, he had just left for Tibet. For a year, I tried unsuccessfully to reach him and was just about to give up when the phone rang one evening. The voice on the line belonged to Rinpoche's attendant. He was calling to say that Rinpoche was about to leave Carmel, which is very near where we live in California. Thankful for the serendipitous phone call, I asked if they would like to rest at our home for the night. That evening, we talked about old times and new, and Rinpoche said he would be happy to contribute to this collection of teachings.

Kongtrul Rinpoche taught the next day at sunrise, stopping sometimes to gaze at the colors staining the early morning sky and the ocean below. Rinpoche is known to be an extraordinary dharma teacher, and I felt very fortunate to hear him teach in person. His self-exploration was extremely moving. Lured into examining my own heart, it seemed as if Kongtrul Rinpoche were saying, "Wake up."

DZIGAR KONGTRUL RINPOCHE

Spiritual Materialism

FIRST, I WOULD LIKE TO SAY that I'm very flattered to be photographed and recorded in this book with such great teachers of the Nyingma tradition. This is a special honor for me because I have received teachings from and have a teacher–student relationship with most of them.

What first comes to mind to speak about is my own spiritual materialism, so let's start there. I find that as I'm reading or reflecting upon the teachings and something becomes clear to me, I immediately want to rush out and teach it to others. Why is this? The answer disturbs me, because although I believe there is a certain amount of good motivation, looking deeply, I discover that actually there is very little intention to help others. Instead, it's all about making an impression, and there is much of my own ego involved. I have become so proficient at disseminating knowledge, particularly the teachings of dharma, that I do it almost automatically. Unconsciously, though, I want to make a good impression on others.

In one sense, because these are dharma teachings, the activity still bears fruit, but in another sense it is quite sad to realize that one is not truly taking the teachings to heart. This is where the impression must be made—on your own heart. If this is not the case, although you might be able to contemplate the dharma, achieve some insight and expound it to others, you will not experience any dramatic change in yourself. So naturally, you cannot instigate significant change in the minds of others, except perhaps in some intellectual capacity.

That, then, is the confession I would like to make. I aspire to be truly free from the entrapment of spiritual materialism. To rid myself of this tendency would bring such long-sought freedom and peace. May I one day practice the dharma without trying to make an impression on others, and instead may I truly make the needed impression on my own heart. My wish should be recorded, so that when I hold a copy of this book in my hand, it will remind my ego of its own spiritual materialism. Now you have to ask me questions.

Perhaps you could speak more about spiritual materialism so that
we can better discern it in ourselves.

I can speak to you about my own knowledge of spiritual materialism, although others might explain it differently. According to my understanding, spiritual materialism is present when the spiritual path is tainted by selfish thoughts or selfish emotions, and we use spiritual practice to

indulge our own ego—to make ourselves look good or to achieve some sort of recognition. You see, because we live closely with others, our paths intermingle. We are so persistently concerned with how our companions will perceive us that we don't know how to be genuine and authentic—to actually be ourselves. Such sensitivity to the opinions of others pervades our dharma activity as well.

Dharma—the teachings of truth spoken by the Buddha Shakyamuni—is completely pure and stainless. Even so, we use it to feed our spiritual materialism. For example, before we even learn the dharma ourselves, we want to enlighten others. Doubtless, there is a certain amount of good intention behind our actions, but again, this often has more to do with the fact that we want to impress others with our breadth of knowledge, our level of realization. In truth, our focus is on the self. The function of self is to promote itself, so if we aren't careful, we can actually turn all of our dharma activity into self-promotion.

We all enjoy being liked and praised.
But it sounds as though pursuing these positive feelings could inhibit the growth of
true spiritual qualities. In our culture, we're accustomed to using pleasant feelings as a
compass to direct our actions; that is, "If it feels right, it must be right." And becoming aware
of our negative qualities is very painful, so it's not instinctual to seek them out.

Yes, we usually judge everything that causes us pain and suffering to be negative and everything that brings us tranquility and happiness to be positive, don't we? But in pursuing happiness and joy and in fleeing pain and suffering, there is an inherent obstacle to our spiritual development, because we are striving to please the ego. Once you truly experience your mind clearly, you will recognize your own spiritual materialism. Such recognition is terribly painful, first because you see that you're acting from that state in the present, and then even more so because you realize that you've been controlled by such tendencies all along and haven't even been aware of it.

Rinpoche, will you please define "ego" according to Vajrayana Buddhism?

The ego is the feeling of self. With this comes the constant need to cherish and protect the self, creating conflicting emotions. For instance, when we get angry, it's because we feel threatened. Anger is a mechanism to protect the "self" that is feeling threatened. Ego is that self which is feeling the threat. Of course, we don't need a dramatic experience such as getting angry for ego to be present. In every situation, there can be a sense of self, either on a subtle, unconscious level or on a gross, more conscious level.

I find it difficult to imagine not having a self. How would this feel?
How would it be different from having a self?

I think one would actually feel great relief and freedom from mental and emotional pain. Of course, there would still be some sense of a self, but it would be different—more of a mental continuum free of ego. You would be able to recognize this by the freedom and the peacefulness of that freedom, by the absence of conflicting emotions and all the suffering they bring. That feeling of peace or lack of it would be a reference point for you to determine to what degree the ego is present. In the words of the Buddha, "When all the errors of mind are exhausted and mind possesses nothing but wisdom, compassion and all positive qualities, that is enlightenment."

Rinpoche, in our immediate reality—today, tomorrow—how can we develop this freedom?

Well, there are many things you can do. What I myself find most helpful is to vigorously counteract ignorance. How? Learn more about your mind. Learn about its functions and its nature. Also, redirect the love and concern you feel for yourself. Turn it toward others and love them as much as you can. Offer them the same compassion you have for yourself. Make a determined effort to thwart the self-cherishing tendency of ego. This will naturally create a gap in your usual patterns of mind and emotions, and in that opening you will see everything in a different light. Then the fears that are self-indulgent will fall away. But you should keep your intelligent fears and actually appreciate them.

Intelligent fears?

It is intelligent to fear your own ignorance and your own ego. It is intelligent to fear your own self-indulgence and negative emotions because of the consequences they may have, not just in this life but also in the next. This intelligent fear is constructive. It will keep you safe. This intelligent fear is your guardian angel.

KHANDRO RINPOCHE

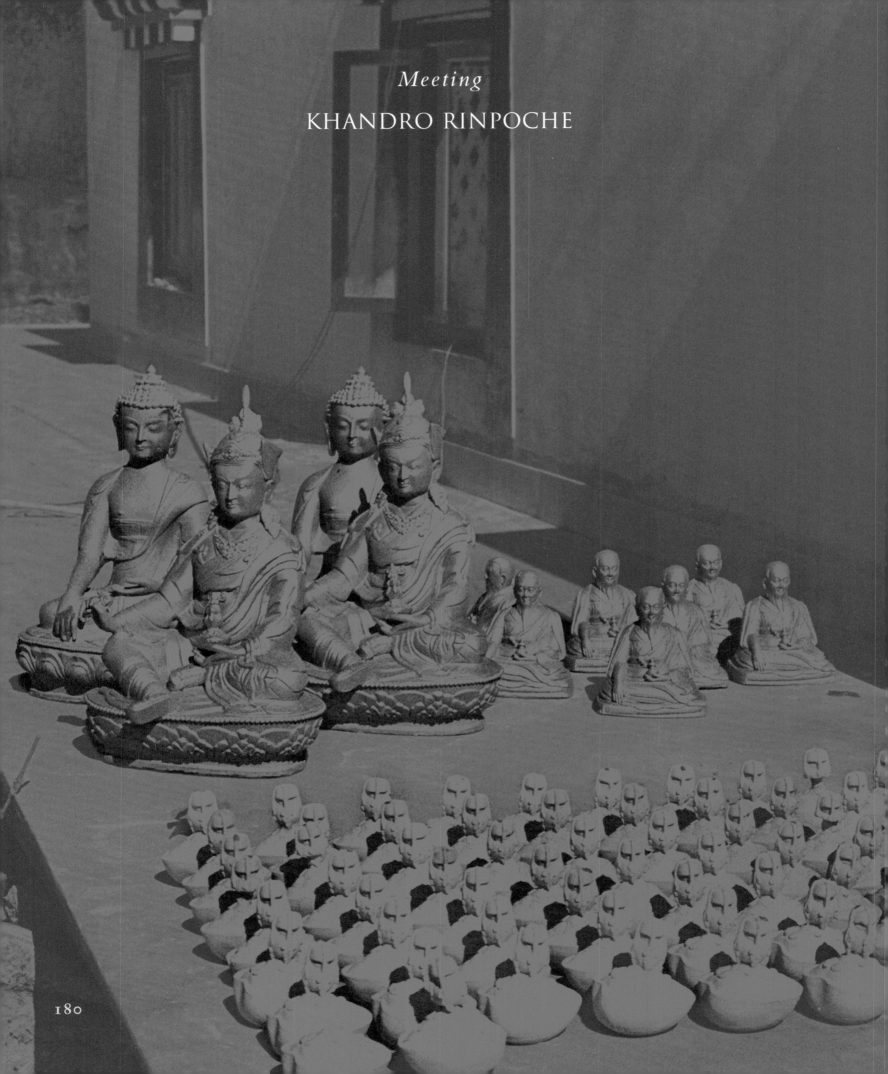

Meeting
KHANDRO RINPOCHE

WHEN I FIRST MET KHANDRO RINPOCHE, she was a young girl translating for her father, Mindroling Trichen Rinpoche. With her clear and resonant speech, she has been expounding the dharma from a very early age, first as her father's English voice and now to her own students in the East and West. In 2001 she was leading a retreat at the Shambhala Mountain Center in Colorado, and I traveled there to request a teaching for this book. In the afternoons I attended the retreat, where Khandro Rinpoche, now a poised and eloquent nun, was teaching a large audience of students.

Until that time, it had not occurred to me that teachings from a female master would be any different in tone, and the question of gender never even came to mind. However, it was apparent during Khandro Rinpoche's afternoon talks that she is often questioned on this subject. A number of students in the group voiced concerns about their identity as women in dharma as well as other women's issues. Though Rinpoche did not invalidate them in any way, she continually and skillfully led us back to the teachings of the Buddha, beyond any concepts of feminine or masculine characteristics.

I next visited Khandro Rinpoche at Samten Tse, her nunnery and retreat center in the Shivalik hills of India. In this remote Himalayan setting, I unexpectedly found myself in the company of lay practitioners, both women and men, and nuns from all over the globe. During lunch, we joined together around a long wooden table for the traditional Indian meal of rice, dahl and curried vegetables. Conversations took place in French, Tibetan, English, Hindi, a medley of accents enlivening the dining hall. Somehow everyone communicated effortlessly, and the good intentions and motivation to practice the dharma were unmistakable. After lunch, Rinpoche called me into her small and elegant shrine room, where she completed her teaching for this book.

Although Rinpoche is quite renowned worldwide, whenever meeting with her privately, I felt immediately engaged and unusually comfortable. Our conversations had a distinct quality—as if they took place in a removed slice of time. She spoke to me with the kind of encouragement that only one woman can give to another, which was especially nourishing when the work on this book seemed never ending. With enthusiasm she said, "When people see the photographs of these great beings, they can receive 'liberation through seeing.'" Those uplifting words stayed in my memory during the completion of the book, and I will remain ever thankful to her.

KHANDRO RINPOCHE

Compassion Is About Awareness

THE BLESSINGS OF OUR GREAT NYINGMA TEACHERS ARE IMMENSE. Simply glimpsing their faces or photographs makes it impossible not to recognize how profound the path of practice is. This recognition involves much more than just having a collection of information or being caught within certain beliefs. It involves genuinely realizing the essence and true meaning behind the teachings of the Buddha, especially as revealed to us through the living examples of our great masters.

This afternoon during the teaching, many people voiced their concerns
about the role of women in Buddhism.

It doesn't really matter whether you are a man or a woman—the essence is not based on gender or on perceived differences between the genders. Yet because of ignorance, your approach to the path is often influenced by your own opinion of who you are. For example, this ignorance might arise when a man identifies with his masculinity and becomes fixated on it. Equally as ignorant would be for a woman to become fixated on her own gender and then, because of her stubborn belief, be unable to see the true and indivisible essence of the teachings. You must decide whether you are going to emphasize your notions of identity or go beyond that ignorance to really understand the essence of dharma, the very heart of the teachings.

It is said that there are teachers like His Holiness Mindroling Trichen Rinpoche, the Karmapa and His Holiness Dilgo Khyentse Rinpoche who can bring about "liberation through seeing"; that is, just seeing these masters can bring about liberation of our concepts. Those who meet them, or even see their image, will not think about whether these teachers are men or women, but rather will sense the immense compassion in their hearts. Anyone can experience the genuine, unbiased kindness of these teachers and be able to take in the blessings of their words.

So although for every woman in Buddhism there are structural developments in progress and special areas we may need to be concerned with, I think it would be more beneficial to focus on transforming the mind and taking the teachings to heart. Rather than concentrating on a small fraction of the totality and magnifying its importance, develop the ability to know the wholeness. That is what dharma practice is about: transforming ignorance and stubbornness into something more flexible and vast. This way, the understanding of dharma deepens within your heart. Then you can truly say, "I have met with these great masters."

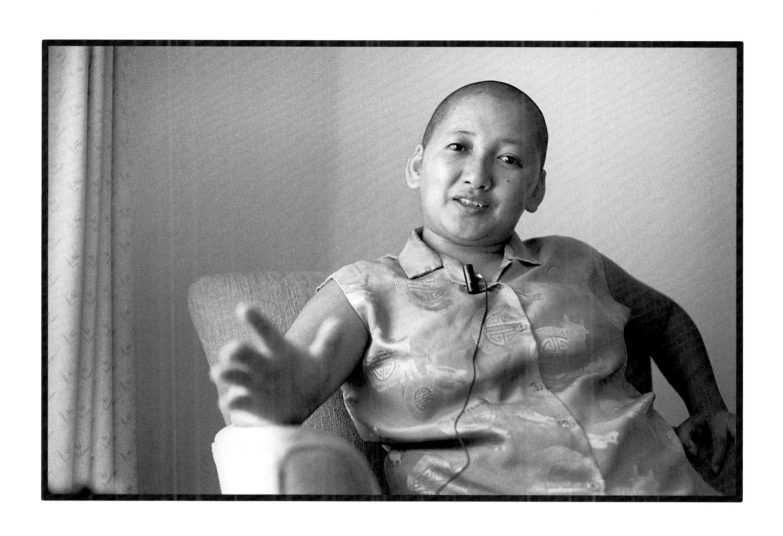

Rinpoche, I'm not sure what you mean when you say "stubbornness."
Will you please give an example?

Stubbornness? We are all perfect examples of that. Stubbornness is anything that holds you up or impedes your progress. Stubbornness is fixating on a certain something that you did not get or that you disagree with. For instance, it could be a preoccupation with lineages, views or matters of tradition. Stubbornness is anything that causes your mind to deviate from the understanding of absolute truth.

How would a preoccupation with view manifest?

It could be like this: "My view is better than yours, my idea is better than yours, your way of attaining realization is inferior to mine." We do that. However, there isn't a concept that is partially ignorant or partially wise. A concept is always a concept. If you hold onto it, no matter how wise it may seem to be, it is not free of ignorance.

Earlier you said we could use logic as a tool to help the mind become more fluid.
Would you please speak about that?

We use logic to examine and dismantle conditioned beliefs so that we are able to realize absolute truth. Logic also develops the eye of discernment. With that eye, we can discriminate between what is true and what is false, allowing us to experience the fundamental ground.

Would we attain liberation at that point?

Liberation does not have to be attained. Liberation is pervasive. Liberation is about being able to let go of things we think are important and actions we think are important. When we are able to cease grasping at false beliefs and concepts, whatever arises spontaneously and naturally is the all-pervasive ground purity.

Rinpoche, within the context of this culture, how do we proceed to develop ourselves?

I notice that sometimes in the West there is a bit too much emphasis on discarding certain things and cultivating others. There seems to be an orientation toward action, and although it may be motivated by a sincere wish for perfection, the action is steeped in criticism toward oneself and others. Rather than imagining that performing an action will resolve our difficulties, we should concentrate on transforming the self. In other words, it is not the external conditions or the search for perfection that we should dwell on. We need to develop openness, vastness, true relaxation and flexibility of mind—not expecting flexibility from others, but instead fostering flexibility within ourselves. If we emphasize inner transformation, the dharma practice we do will be much more beneficial. This is true not only in the West but everywhere.

There are so many teachings about love and compassion,
and I trust in them. But why does compassion actually work? Is there logic behind it?
Would you talk about what true compassion is?

Compassion is not about kindness. Compassion is about awareness. Compassion in the general sense of kindness would be an expression of awareness, but one that might not necessarily be free from the stain of ego grasping. Genuine compassion is egoless. It is the inherent essence expressed, inseparable from awareness. This natural essence, which is genuine compassion, does not need to be formulated or even expressed as something like "compassion." We see this exemplified in our great teachers. Their genuine compassion does not require phrases and expressions or even actions. Just their presence, who they are, is nothing other than the quintessence of compassion. We, in contrast, have to invent and demonstrate compassion. Our contaminated compassion still requires effort and deliberation. That is conventional or general compassion.

But isn't it still of some benefit to practice this conventional compassion?

It's better than nothing.

If we practiced this kind of conventional, ego-tainted compassion repeatedly,
would that lead to awareness compassion?

Yes. The good thing about the use of deliberate or conventional compassion is that it matures the mind so that ego grasping diminishes. It definitely has that effect and is therefore a skillful method for developing awareness compassion.

So the logic of compassion is that even when initially tainted with self,
it still leads us to our intrinsic nature?

Right. That's very right.

So what we're practicing is an imitation of the true nature…

…of compassion so that it becomes familiar and eventually becomes our natural instinct, no longer requiring deliberation.

Rinpoche, I heard you compare our search for the ground of compassion to peeling an onion.

Yes, the onion is a useful analogy. We may think that if we peel away enough of its outer layers, a core which is the real onion will be revealed. But when all the layers are removed, there is no substance we can call "onion." Still, in order to make this discovery, we have to go through the process of peeling. As long as we are hesitant, thinking that there might be something tangible beyond the next layer, we have to take the conventional approach of peeling the onion. So we continue exploring, saying, "Let's peel off the next layer. What is there?" until an irreversible confidence in emptiness arises, and we are no longer haunted by the thought that maybe there is an onion after all.

The haunting onion.… The word "emptiness" is so difficult to relate to, Rinpoche. Are there other English words that might convey the meaning?

Other than "emptiness"? Actually, I would much rather use "the absolute true nature."

And all of us have this inherent purity, the absolute true nature?

Right. But the absolute true nature is all-pervasive. It cannot be divided. It would be incorrect to impose a structure and refer to absolute truth as being within you or within me as if there were two separate absolute truths. Our understanding of the word "all" can be misleading. In this case, it is wrong to think of "all" as a gathering or compilation. Therefore, simply leave it like this: "absolute truth."

Thank you, Rinpoche. This afternoon, you were talking about looking into or through the eyes of others. Would you speak more about that?

We talk about compassion but in a very impersonal way. Genuine compassion arises as the ability to go beyond self. This requires that we transcend our preoccupation with our own happiness and suffering. As meditators, one of the first things we can do is to honestly look at the world from behind another's eyes. Experience that person's craving for happiness and fear of suffering with the same immediacy that we would if his heart and mind were ours. We may see that this individual's immense hope and fear are even greater than our own. See the similarities we all share. We cannot even begin to commit ourselves to the path of selfless compassion if our mind is unable to sense the sameness of the ground we all stand upon. Ultimately, to understand selflessness, we have to go beyond self.

This breaks down some of the imaginary barriers between us?

And can also lead to the understanding of all-pervasive ground, an understanding that "Oh, yes, there is the same happiness, the same suffering, the same ignorance and the same wisdom." And yet this mind of ours thinks, "No, it is different. Your problem is your problem, my problem is my problem." And so separation begins. When that separation is established, we definitely have a natural instinct to safeguard our own selfish interests and to be unaware of others' needs.

But if we were able to really look into the eyes of another, we would see the oneness of all sentient beings and the sameness of the ground we all share. And then we would know the immense potential each being has for complete liberation at that very moment.

JIGME KHYENTSE RINPOCHE

Meeting

JIGME KHYENTSE RINPOCHE

I USED TO CATCH GLIMPSES OF JIGME KHYENTSE RINPOCHE IN DORDOGNE as he sat before Kyabje Dilgo Khyentse Rinpoche's statuesque form. It wasn't until he visited Canada in 2002, however, that I had the opportunity to receive teachings from him. He had come to teach the *Bodhicaryavatara* with Dzongsar Khyentse Rinpoche.

As I waited for Rinpoche's talk in Vancouver to begin, a friend arrived with her very sweet but very large dog, Shadow, in tow. Shadow settled noisily on the floor, stretched out and let out a loud, satisfied yawn. I was utterly distracted and wondered why her canine friend had chosen to sit by me. Settling my mind in preparation for the teaching seemed impossible, and my irritation was overflowing.

Then Jigme Khyentse Rinpoche began to speak. And the first thing he said was "Nondistraction is the path. But when I try to practice it and it doesn't work, it annoys me—that's what keeps me hooked in samsara. And when I hear something irritating, all my romantic ideas of 'equal rights' go right down the drain. Isn't it amazing how annoyed we are by even the smallest thing?" With his words, my agitation dissolved into amusement.

Throughout the teaching, Rinpoche captured our common foibles in the spotlight of his slightly acerbic humor, yet the moderation of his deep kindness made the exposure somehow comforting and delightful. At one point Rinpoche referred to an Academy Award–winning film, saying, "To what extent do we really want to be like Leonardo DiCaprio? After all, *Titanic* was just a ship-wreck. We are so ready to model ourselves after some Hollywood star, to look like one and live like one. But why not model ourselves after bodhisattvas like Shantideva? Why not strive to look like them and live like them?" I had not heard a Tibetan master teach in quite the same way, and throughout the afternoon my attention never wavered.

Later that day I asked Rinpoche if he would contribute to this book. He agreed to do so and gave the teaching that follows. Although Rinpoche is quite witty, he is known as a formidable scholar, and during our sessions the environment was one of serious dharma study. He taught over several days, at times in a high-rise apartment filled with modern artwork and the smoky scent of Tibetan incense, his gaze directed at the clear Vancouver sky. Another day, he continued the teachings behind a thin partition at the public venue, with hundreds of people milling about and talking loudly outside. Still, the power of his speech was such that, again, distraction was absent. I am immensely grateful that Jigme Khyentse Rinpoche kindly agreed to have his inimitable teaching included here.

JIGME KHYENTSE RINPOCHE

Why Did the Buddha Teach?

*Rinpoche, English-speaking students often mention the "nature of mind" teachings.
I wonder if you would speak about this.*

IT'S COMMON THESE DAYS TO HEAR ABOUT TEACHINGS ON THE NATURE OF THE MIND. Most Buddhist books and brochures seem to mention these instructions. Many students are interested in practicing them, and I too would like to practice them. The problem is that one tends to romanticize "nature of mind" advice, thinking it offers "gain without pain." This is too easy and something of a misconception. I think the "nature of mind" teachings actually require a true ability to meditate and tame the mind. Buddhism provides us with myriad effective methods for transforming our minds. But even after receiving many teachings, for some reason we are often still unaffected. Or perhaps I should say that, in my own case, my mind is not easily affected by them.

Why do you say that, Rinpoche?

Well, because I'm not interested enough. Although I have complete faith in the authenticity of the teachings and absolute confidence in my great masters, having received invaluable teachings from Khyentse Rinpoche, Dudjom Rinpoche, Kangyur Rinpoche and many others, nevertheless, when it actually comes to allowing them to influence my mind, I seldom do because sources of distraction provide tremendous competition. For example, there is a romantic part of me that thinks of the path as being like a movie. When I watch a movie and am entertained, I often have no idea of whether or not it is a good film. Frankly, if a movie distracts me successfully, I like it, and if it doesn't, I don't. The criterion is the degree of distraction, not the quality of the film. And I seem to have the same romantic approach on the path.

But when Lord Buddha taught, it was not in order to entertain us. He had no intention of selling anything. To put it plainly, in the Four Truths the Buddha was teaching about suffering. He didn't look for politically correct words and say, "First truth: pleasurably challenged; second truth: emotionally challenged." The Buddha didn't have to do that. He put the truth of suffering clearly. He said, "You are suffering, and there is a way out."

Regarding why I myself turn to my teachers and the path, it's not because they're entertaining, and it's not only because the dharma is interesting. It's because I have no other way out. Training the mind is the way out. We begin by renouncing what does not fit with our spiritual

aspirations, that is, our negative emotions (or impractical emotions, if you don't like the word "negative.") Our minds have many impractical habits, starting with ignorance, attachment or lust, and aggression. For example, being obsessed by something is not pleasant and is impractical. We might enjoy being in love, but being *hopelessly* in love is impractical. Obsessively hating someone or something is impractical. Extreme emotions simply do not support our well-being or our aspirations on the path. And that is why we need to train our minds.

To train our minds successfully, we must cultivate diligence and concentration. Normally, we just eat, sleep and distract ourselves, but we can foster diligence by giving this mind of ours some measure of discipline, some concentration and by not letting it roam indiscriminately wherever it pleases. In fact, perhaps just the act of watching our minds for one moment is in itself a discipline. For example, if we can catch those instants when we think, "Maybe I should go out" or "Maybe I should sit and meditate," we have a way of developing discipline, because right there, in those very moments of decision, is where the potential for freedom or distraction lies.

You'll notice as we sit here now we're thinking of a multitude of things. But if we become aware of our minds' distractions even for a moment, that is what is meant by "setting the mind in concentration." If we don't grasp the moment, the mind is lured away to do its usual thing. It follows what it likes and fights what it doesn't like. I can't speak for you, but my mind is involved in only one of two occupations; it either raves about something or criticizes something. It either likes or dislikes.

We are torn between such likes and dislikes. Like wild animals or cannibals, our emotions eat our happiness away. We are constantly haunted by the fear of not having what we want or getting what we don't want. If we don't manage to discipline our minds and guard them from distraction, experiencing these wild emotions is our only alternative.

Sometimes we equate happiness with having the freedom to express our emotions.

Yes, and we tend to think we are freely expressive, free-thinking individuals, but how free are we really? If we have the freedom to be happy, then why aren't we?

Are you happy, Rinpoche?

I have every reason to be happy, but actually whether or not I am happy depends upon this thing called "me," my mind. And if this mind will not stay calm for even one instant, how can I be happy and free from disturbing emotions? Again, if we can grasp this mind for a few moments—not the "nature of mind," just our daily mind—and not fall prey to publicists and marketing strategists and so on, then freedom and happiness may be possible.

We are told that this freedom of mind is actually right here with us, and yet it's so difficult to find. We can't buy it. We can't secure it with insurance policies. Power and wealth do not bring it to us. This freedom is like a hidden gold mine, and we are like beggars who live in a shack directly above it. We beggars don't know there is a wealth of gold beneath our dwelling, and so we spend all our time in the streets searching for sustenance. The gold doesn't say, "I am here. Dig me up. You'll be rich." In the same way, enlightenment will not come to us unless we apply discipline and concentration to this discursive mind of ours. If we just sit here and wish, "May I get enlightened," it's not going to happen.

> *But Rinpoche, hearing about this freedom, knowing it is there,*
> *or even glimpsing it doesn't seem to be enough.*

Yes, when we wake up, we need to stay awake. To do so, we need to meditate. We sentient beings have been hibernating for a very long time—so long that we don't know how to keep ourselves awake. Keeping awake requires repetitive rousing. Imagine you are using an alarm clock with a snooze button, but here the snooze button isn't permission to go back to sleep; it's a repeated reminder to meditate and stay awake.

There is one more point I would like to make: we need to maintain perspective on why we are practicing, so that we are not shocked when our emotions arise in response to difficulties on the path. If our minds were already flawlessly trained, we wouldn't need to be making any effort now. Even though being perfect is what we aspire to, it's imperative not to let our expectations of perfection obstruct our training.

> As long as space endures,
> As long as there are beings to be found,
> May I continue likewise to remain
> To drive away the sorrows of the world.

SHECHEN RABJAM RINPOCHE

Meeting

SHECHEN RABJAM RINPOCHE

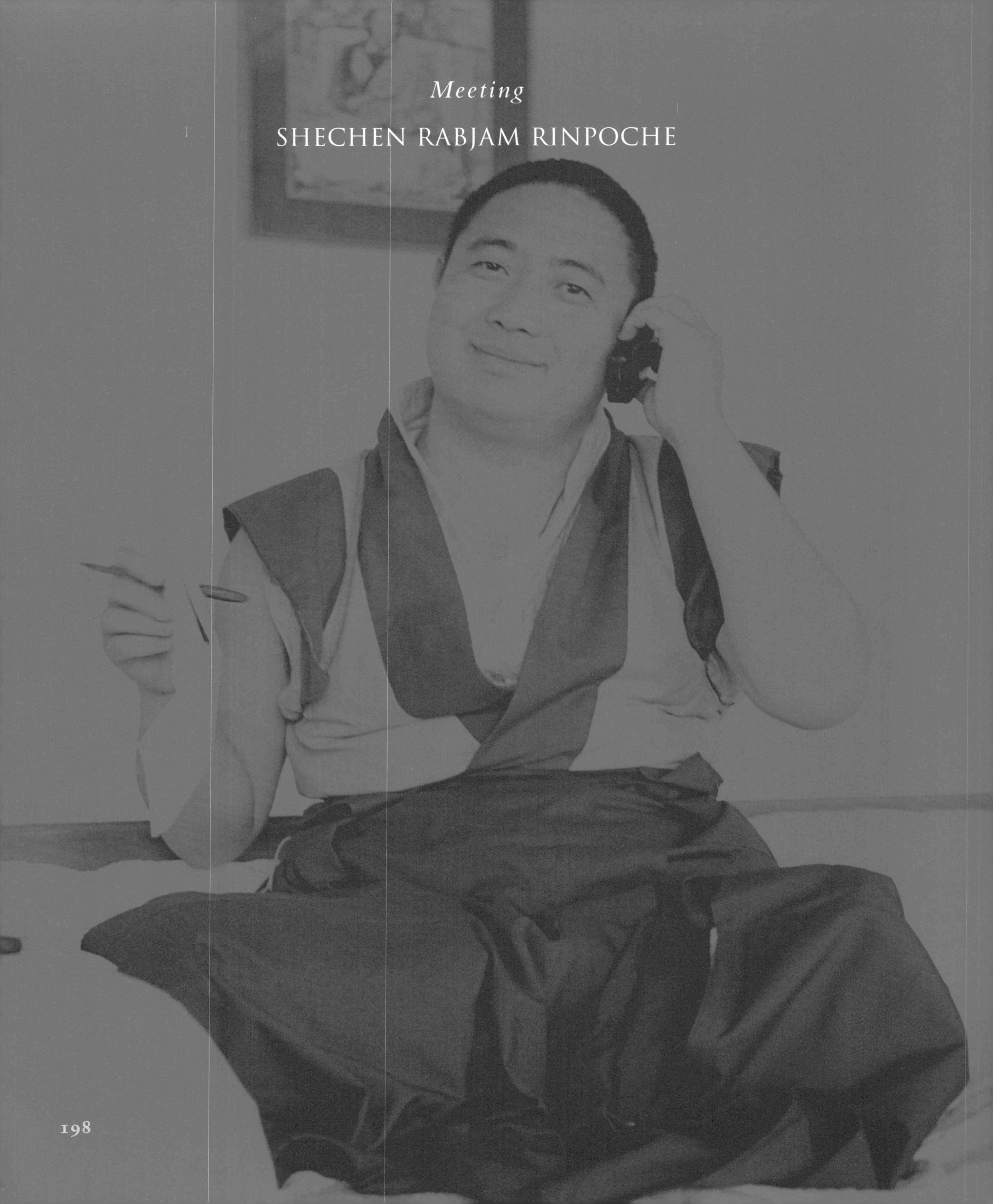

Whᴇɴ ᴡᴇ ꜰɪʀꜱᴛ ʟɪᴠᴇᴅ ɪɴ Nᴇᴘᴀʟ ᴅᴜʀɪɴɢ ᴛʜᴇ ʟᴀᴛᴇ ꜱᴇᴠᴇɴᴛɪᴇꜱ, Rabjam Rinpoche was in his teenage years and was receiving instruction in Buddhist studies from his grandfather, Dilgo Khyentse Rinpoche. From the age of five until the passing of His Holiness in 1991, Rabjam Rinpoche stayed with him continuously, receiving every teaching he gave. Now, he holds responsibility for all of Dilgo Khyentse Rinpoche's monasteries in Nepal, Tibet and Bhutan and works tirelessly to fulfill his grandfather's aspirations. Under Rabjam Rinpoche's direction, Shechen Monastery in Nepal is a flourishing and expansive center of Buddhist training and practice.

On the day in 2001 that I went to request a teaching from Rinpoche for this book, it became obvious how long it had been since I had explored the lanes surrounding Boudha stupa. Although we used to live just steps away from Shechen Monastery, the back streets of Boudhanath were now disorienting. The burst of construction in recent years had turned our old neighborhood into a labyrinth of narrow alleys flanked by the tall concrete walls of new monasteries, and I had to ask for directions every few hundred yards. Shechen Monastery was unrecognizable at first because it had grown to such an astounding degree.

My memories of Dilgo Khyentse Rinpoche were exceptionally vivid that day. I heard the same sounds of Tibetan monks chanting, saw the hundreds of shoes lined up outside his prayer hall, tasted the Boudha dust in my mouth just like so many years ago. Walking up the steps to the monastery, I longingly wished that His Holiness were still there and I could prostrate to his wondrous, noble form once again.

I waited for Rabjam Rinpoche in one of the monastery's large halls adjacent to his open greeting room. Against one wall was a stupa, holding relics of Kyabje Khyentse Rinpoche. The reliquary was set with semiprecious stones and surrounded by offerings. The flames of dozens of butter lamps were reflected in the stupa's golden surface; garlands of marigolds draped the shrine in fragrant saffron waves; the scent of incense conquered the air. The cadenced drums and horns of Buddhist ceremonies and the chanting of hundreds of monks reverberating in the background brought to mind what an amazing example Shechen Monastery is of the resiliency and vibrancy of the Nyingmapas.

I passed the time watching very diverse groups of visitors stream in and out of Rabjam Rinpoche's greeting room. First to call on Rinpoche were members of the royal family of Bhutan, who were quickly ushered in to his sitting room. They sat on the floor and spoke with Rinpoche in hushed tones. Next, there came a clan of Tibetan nomads in heavy woolen robes. Their long hair was in braids and big nuggets of turquoise hung like cracked sky around their necks. They had come very far to receive initiations and teachings. Bowing low at the waist with their palms together in respect, they carefully pulled silky white scarves from the folds of their robes to offer to Rinpoche. Following them, a party of thirty businessmen entered, dressed in suits and ties, briefcases reverently held at their knees as they went to receive his blessings. They kneeled on the floor of Rinpoche's room while he gave an oral transmission.

After a most interesting and peaceful wait, an attendant led me to a private sitting room where I met Rinpoche for the first time in many years. In his exceptionally kind and gentle manner, Rabjam Rinpoche generously spoke the words that follow.

SHECHEN RABJAM RINPOCHE

Freeing Ourselves from Suffering

*Rinpoche, in Tibetan Buddhism, we are often reminded of the value
of being born as a human. But for those who aren't familiar with the idea of reincarnation,
"precious human birth" might be a new concept. Would you please discuss this?*

YES. THE FIRST, MOST FORTUNATE CONDITION FOR PROGRESSING TO ENLIGHTENMENT is being born into this human existence or human body. Such existence does not just come about spontaneously of its own accord. Lord Buddha says in the scriptures that it comes from having observed a spiritual discipline in former lives. This existence we now have is a reflection of our own exertion in past lives and is quite a unique opportunity for traveling the path all the way to enlightenment. We must appreciate its value and not squander this remarkable opportunity by living only for survival's sake.

We can consider this human existence to be like a ship that can sail to any destination. It can go to very beautiful places or to places of deep suffering. This depends entirely upon us. We can use this human existence positively, gradually bringing ourselves to liberation and enlightenment, or we can use it to accumulate great negativity, predisposing ourselves to a lower type of existence. People often ask me, "What is the meaning of my life?" or "What should I do with my life?" It seems to me the most fruitful thing we can do with our lives is to free ourselves from the suffering inherent in samsara and embark on the path toward full enlightenment in order to free other beings from suffering. That is definitely the best thing we can do.

*It's so easy to become entangled in worldly responsibilities and seemingly endless complications.
How do we go about freeing ourselves and what do we need for this endeavor?*

It seems that rather than avoiding suffering, we are always running toward it, and rather than achieving happiness, we are turning our backs on it. Unwittingly, we contradict our own aspirations by the way we act and think and speak. Why? This certainly is not our wish, but we don't know how to use our opportunities. That is why we say that having a spiritual teacher is a favorable and necessary circumstance. In order to achieve our goals, we need someone to help us discern what ought to be accomplished and what ought to be avoided. That someone has to have wisdom; that someone is very precious and is called the "perfect teacher." So when our goal is liberation, we must search for and find this perfect teacher, seek advice and put it into practice. Spiritual teachers are like guides whose function is to show us the path by means of their profound experience and realization.

From where does this profound realization come? From an authentic lineage, whose methods of achieving enlightenment have been verified over time. The favorable condition of having a spiritual teacher rests on both a vast treasury of past transmission and on the present authentic realization of the person holding that lineage. This is quite different from some new religions or New Age varieties of spirituality, which are created and promoted by a mere individual. Because those paths are completely new, there is no true indication of whether or not they can lead people to liberation and enlightenment. It is all speculative. And so it is better for us to rely upon a proven lineage and authentic spiritual friend who can show us the way. But remember, as the Buddha said, "I have shown you the path; it is up to you to travel it."

According to the "Four Considerations," first we should see ourselves as a sick person who needs help, who needs to be healed. In the same way that a person has to recognize his illness before seeking a cure, we must accept the fact that we are in need of aid, that the practice of dharma is a necessity. We should think of the teacher as a skilled physician who can diagnose our illness and advise us as to a cure. We can look upon the master's instructions as the prescription and consider our practice of the dharma to be the medicine and treatment that will heal us.

In order for us to be "cured," in order for us to achieve progress on the path, a supporting structure must be established. This framework is provided by the three trainings that form the basis of the Buddhist path: discipline, concentration and wisdom. In the beginning, we are enveloped in the darkness of ignorance, a profound lack of awareness. This ignorance or confusion is the main cause of samsara, and it must be dispelled if we want to free ourselves from suffering. To do so, we need wisdom. Yet the light of wisdom will not come about instantaneously. First, we must listen to and study the teachings, then deeply contemplate their meaning. Once we have grasped the meaning, we must integrate it into our mindstream; this is what we call "familiarization" or meditation.

But wisdom will not come about if our minds are constantly distracted and scattered. It needs to be based on clear, well-focused and stable concentration. Likewise, we cannot achieve proper concentration if our behavior—the activities of our body, speech and mind—is completely wild. This is why concentration itself needs to be grounded in self-discipline; we must have a certain amount of control over our activities. In this way, it becomes clear that we need to train in discipline first, then develop the ability to focus one-pointedly on the object of our meditation, which will finally lead to the flourishing of wisdom.

*Rinpoche, earlier you spoke about enlightenment as our primary goal.
In English, the word "enlightenment" is used in many ways and sometimes simply implies
vague spiritual understanding. For the sake of clarity, can you define the word
according to Vajrayana Buddhism?*

Enlightenment is the realization of absolute truth regarding the true nature of phenomena. This means both outer phenomena and the inner phenomena of one's mind. We can call that realization buddhahood.

In contrast, ego is the perception of an ordinary or unrealized being. But actually, we find there is no ego. Ordinary beings perceive outer phenomena as having intrinsic existence and solidity. But again, upon careful examination, phenomena can be seen to have no solid, autonomous existence and are ungraspable. So the way we ordinary beings perceive things is at odds with the way things actually are. Hence, the goal of the path is precisely this: to see things just as they are and not simply the way they appear to our minds.

Thank you very much for taking the time to give these teachings, Rinpoche.

I have just spoken a few words that came to mind. These reflections have been helpful to me and perhaps will be to you as well. In any case, if you find what I have said useful, then reflect upon it and bring it into your own experience. If not, you don't have to worry.

NAMKHAI NYINGPO RINPOCHE

Meeting
NAMKHAI NYINGPO RINPOCHE

THE UNSPOILED KINGDOM OF BHUTAN is a country in which the predominant religion is Vajrayana Buddhism. Only in the past twenty-five years has Bhutan welcomed a limited number of tourists, and when we first moved to the East, her closed borders were alluring and mysterious. While living in Nepal, we met many Bhutanese yogis and monks who came to study with Buddhist masters in Kathmandu. Sometimes they would tell me stories of their country. Although Bhutan is not large, the many holy places of pilgrimage and the depth of Bhutanese devotion to dharma they described always made it sound like a vast place. And although many different dialects are spoken there, the language of Vajrayana Buddhism reaches from border to border.

Namkhai Nyingpo Rinpoche generally stays in his monastery in eastern Bhutan, spending much time in retreat. In addition to Lodrak Kharchu Dudjomling in Bhutan, he has a monastery in Lodrak, Tibet, a seven-day walk from Lhasa. A friend called me one day in 1998 to say that Rinpoche was visiting the United States for the first time, and we decided to organize an impromptu teaching at my home in California for the next weekend.

We notified only a few people of the event and told them that, because of limited parking space, we would shuttle them from a nearby market. We planned on making only two or three trips, but every time I drove back to the store, there was another group of five or six students holding red meditation cushions under their arms. The patrons of the very upscale market looked at them questioningly; fortunately no one complained. We anticipated no more than twenty participants, but by the time we had finished shuttling everyone, eighty pairs of shoes were lined up on the front porch of the house and the living room was full.

Since most of the students present had been studying dharma for some time, Rinpoche addressed his teachings to these older practitioners. As he spoke, the room seemed to flood with his very light, very present being. It was as though he had transported the energy from his monastery far away in eastern Bhutan to our ordinary California abode. The words of his teaching were bracing for many of us. Rinpoche gave a solemn but invigorating talk, emphasizing that each of us is responsible for remembering everything our teachers have given to us. Using subtle examples of how important the teacher–student relationship is to himself, Rinpoche demonstrated that even on higher stages of the path, the guru is the hub from which all progress radiates.

All of us were deeply affected by Rinpoche's teaching, by his logical words of encouragement, inspiring us to reevaluate our priorities. After Rinpoche left that evening, some of us reflected upon our life in the West and how easily we are controlled by worldly tasks, our existence becoming one "big errand" and time slipping by beneath the radar of our limited awareness. Everyone hoped for Rinpoche's rapid return.

That weekend I asked Namkhai Nyingpo Rinpoche to contribute to this book, and he later gave the teaching that follows.

NAMKHAI NYINGPO RINPOCHE

Precious Time

IT IS VERY IMPORTANT FOR US TO CONSIDER HOW WE ARE USING OUR TIME IN THIS LIFE. Many of us spend the whole day being constantly busy; then when we go home at night, we can't even fall asleep. There is no moment during our hectic existence when we are able to take a break from all the commotion and truly be at rest. There is endless activity. Why do we go along with this routine? So that we will be successful, earn money and obtain what we think we need to get by. We act as if our mundane concerns had great meaning, but upon reflection, in fact they have no particularly deep purpose. As it turns out, after all this busyness, the time arrives when we die. At the moment of death, we can't take any souvenirs of ordinary life with us. The only thing we will carry into the next life is our own karma.

Yet karma seems almost invisible.
It's quite difficult to remember to take responsibility for something we can't see.
How can we better understand karma and the consequences of our actions?

Any explanation of karma is, in fact, extremely subtle. Jigme Lingpa used this metaphor: when a bird flies high in the sky, no shadow is seen; only as the bird nears the earth does it appear. Karma has the same dynamic. As we move through this lifetime, we don't see our own karma. But at a later date our karma, our shadow, becomes quite evident. We must remember that the problems and suffering in our lives don't just appear like surprises falling out of the sky without any causes or conditions. The suffering that we experience is not something that another person has given to us or created. Suffering does not arise in that way.

What is the creator of karma? Who is the creator of karma? If we search for the source, we find it to be the mind. Karma depends upon the mental attitude that accompanies our actions. When we experience suffering, it is because negative karma that we have created in past lives is now ripening. This is why we say we must master our own mind.

In the present, we must think about what we wish to take with us into future lives. For instance, if we use our prosperity during this lifetime to make offerings to the Three Jewels or to help those less fortunate than ourselves, we are making very wise use of our wealth. If we practice such generosity, then when we die, we will have something to carry from this life to the next— our virtuous activity. It is up to us right now to create the positive conditions that will allow us

to have advantageous situations in the future. Advantageous situations in the future depend upon creating positive conditions right now. I advise you, please practice. Please train your mind. It is so very important.

A story about Katyayana, one of the great disciples of the Buddha, is an excellent illustration. Katyayana was invited one morning to a great king's palace, where he was entertained with music and dance all day long. At the end of the festivities, the king asked Katyayana if he had enjoyed the entertainment. Katyayana said, "Was there entertainment? I didn't see anything at all." This was because Katyayana had allowed his mind to remain in a state of meditation.

However, the king did not believe him, so Katyayana asked the king to summon a prisoner from the dungeon and entertain him with music and dance the following day. He told the king, "Give the prisoner a container filled to the brim with oil. Tell him he must carry it around the banquet hall all day without spilling a drop, or he will be killed on the spot." The king did as he was asked, and the prisoner spent the next day carefully circling the hall. None of the oil was spilled. Why? Because he didn't look to the right or the left. The king asked the prisoner if he had enjoyed the entertainment, but the prisoner had been so focused on his task that he too had seen nothing.

Katyayana asked the king, "Do you understand now? This man didn't observe any of the festivities because he was worried about being executed and so was tremendously vigilant. Similarly, I did not perceive the entertainment because I am afraid of being reborn within the wheel of life. That is why I pay so much attention to my meditation." In the same way, not allowing ourselves to be distracted, we must bring such vigilance and focus to our own practice.

Thank you, Rinpoche. Before you return to Bhutan,
is there any particular advice you wish to give the readers of this book?

At present, those of us who enjoy the good fortune of having met the sacred teachings of Buddhism must not waste this human life in meaningless acts. We must live so that at the time of death we find ourselves without regret and able to experience joy and happiness in complete freedom. Please consider this.

Moreover, during this lifetime, please apply the profound teachings you have received from qualified spiritual guides to your own mind and practice them as much as possible. If you do not do so and instead allow your mind to swell with pride, the eight worldly concerns will drive you to teach Buddhism to others or to write books about it. None of this will be helpful at the time of death. Instead, you must rely on the positive influence of mindfulness to overcome your own faults, to train in impartial pure vision and to continually meditate on love, compassion and the mind of awakening in relation to all sentient beings. Regard your kind spiritual master as greater than the Buddha, and with intense devotion make union with the spiritual master's mind the sole point of your dharma practice. If you do, the master's blessings will enter your mind. It has been said that such blessings will completely defeat the negative force of any outer or inner obstacles and will cause realization to arise effortlessly and spontaneously. I ask you to please consider this and to practice accordingly.

DR. TROGAWA RINPOCHE

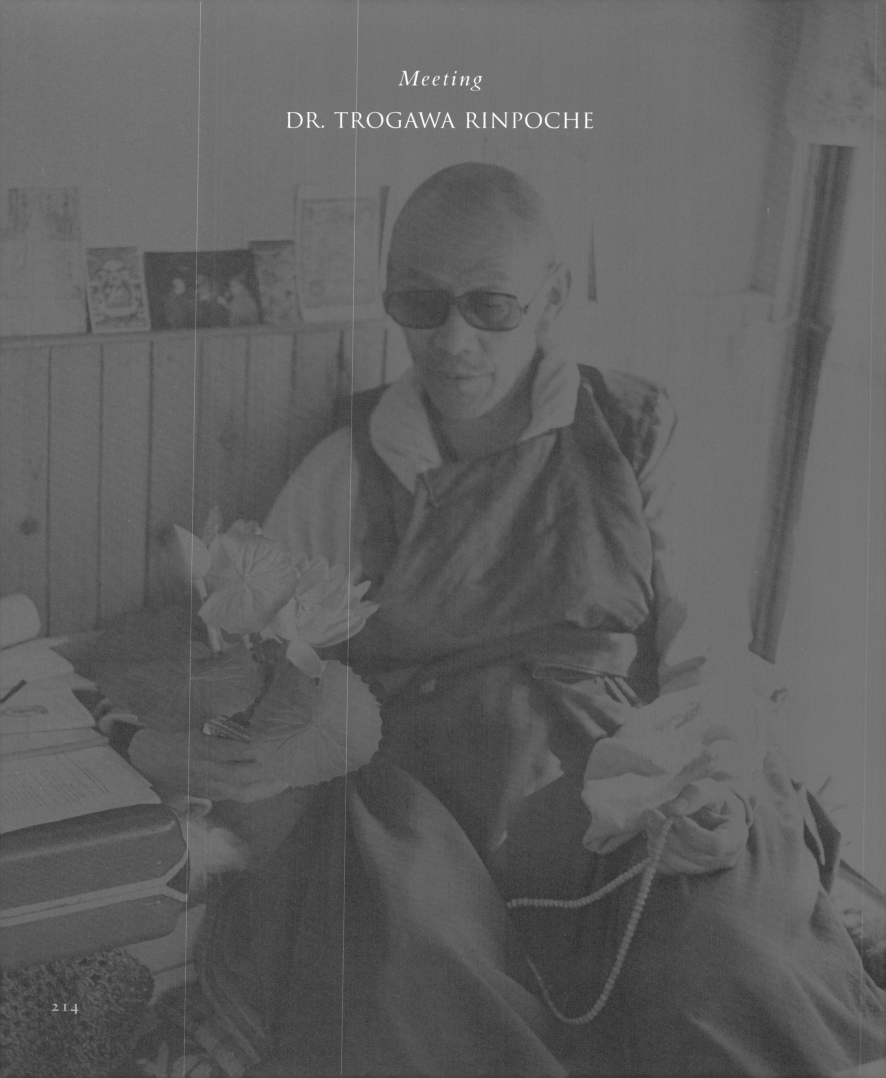

Meeting

DR. TROGAWA RINPOCHE

THE PRACTICE OF MEDICINE IN THE TIBETAN TRADITION IS HOLISTIC, taking into consideration not only the physical but also the mental and spiritual state of the individual. Dr. Trogawa Rinpoche is a Nyingma lama and a highly respected physician in the Tibetan community. During the years we lived in the East, Rinpoche was our family doctor and treated every illness with astonishing efficacy. When we returned to America to live, no longer having access to Rinpoche's care was a true loss. Fortunately, Dr. Trogawa eventually visited the United States in the late 1980s, where he saw patients and gave a comprehensive teaching at the Shambhala Center in Berkeley, California. There, he explained the link between spiritual practice and both physical and mental health. In assembling this book, I had hoped Rinpoche might give a similar teaching here.

To ask him, I had to travel to his clinic in Darjeeling, a hill station in northern India that is the site of many Tibetan Buddhist monasteries. In the year 2000, I flew to Nepal to meet up with my friend Penzom Lama. Along with a handful of trekkers, we took a small plane to Bagdogra, in the humid, subtropical region known as the Terai, the flatlands of Nepal. We landed in what appeared to be a cowfield, empty except for a small shack and a few gypsy cabs that had come to greet the plane. We hired one of them to take us to the Indian border. Stepping over the border from one country to the next has a magical feeling; everything changes with that one step—the language, the customs, the manners, the spices and in this case the colors of the women's silk and cotton saris.

Going through customs was like being in a slow-motion movie with a very loud soundtrack. When finally over the border, we rented a battered Land Rover for the remainder of the trip. The area is full of these four-wheel-drive vehicles that have been kept in basic working order since the British abandoned them in the 1940s. Some are more decrepit than others.

We ascended quickly from the sweltering plains into the mountains of northern India where Darjeeling sits at an elevation of more than seven thousand feet. As we drove along scores of switchbacks, the weather shifted and we met dense fog, sheets of rain and eventually hailstones. On either side of the pavement, the road gave way to sheer cliffs that seemed to fall hundreds of feet down.

Our Sikh driver was relaxed in spite of the inclement conditions and noisy roar of the old engine. His door kept falling open, startling us and filling the car with moist air. I asked him, "Please, can't you make your door stay closed? It's dangerous." He would slam it shut, adjust his pink turban, and turn his head around to speak, saying, "Not to worry, Madam. It is only my door that is opening that way. Not yours. No problem." As long as he doesn't fall out, I thought to myself and stopped my talking, hoping he would keep his eyes on the road. The journey felt interminable.

The air became thinner as we climbed, and acres of tea crops gave way to a forest of firs and pines. Wild flowering vines climbed everywhere, nourished by the damp mist and clean air. Darjeeling itself seems to grow naturally out of the landscape with structures built along the steep slopes of the terrain. The town is somewhat reminiscent of the British under whose occupancy the region was first developed. Prayer flags and monasteries are interspersed with formal boarding schools housed in old stone manors, where the more privileged Indian, Nepalese and Bhutanese educate their children. English cottages bordered by rose gardens seem to have been lifted from Great Britain, and still-grand tea plantations surround the town. The hotel where we stayed was furnished with faded English antiques and offered afternoon tea replete with dainty cucumber sandwiches. The lobby walls were painted a deep burgundy and lined with ornate Tibetan thangkas depicting Buddhist deities. We rested there for the night.

The next morning, we went to Chagpori Tibetan Medical Institute, Trogawa Rinpoche's clinic, medical school and home. Only a discreet sign and prayer flags flying from the roof and walls identified the yellow building. As we entered, I recalled how Rinpoche had talked about establishing a school of Tibetan medicine when I had first seen him in Kathmandu. Now here we were.

It had been many years since Rinpoche had given me a check-up, so I requested one before his teaching. He took my pulse, which is one of the primary methods of diagnosis in Tibetan medicine. Rinpoche's movements are so unusually light and fluid that his hands appeared to float to my wrist. Somehow he is able to read one's physical condition as if it were clearly inscribed in the beat of the heart and flow of the blood. People say his medicine and advice have cured many ailments that other doctors could not address, and this has been my experience as well.

After the examination, Rinpoche directed us into the shrine room next door so that I could photograph him. At first he playfully covered himself in a blanket, as if hiding, and said in Tibetan, "Okay, this should be a good photo." He did, however, eventually reveal his face to give the teaching. Rinpoche's uplifting words give a sense of the capacity each of us has to sustain and nurture our own physical and mental well-being.

DR. TROGAWA RINPOCHE

Maintaining Balance in Body and Mind

IN ACCORDANCE WITH TIBETAN TRADITION, I would first like to greet you and the readers of this book. *Tashi delek!*

Tashi delek, Rinpoche. Many of us are struggling to maintain good health during these times. Will you give us some advice from the Tibetan medical point of view?

I can give a brief summary, and then you can ask me questions if you like. First, it is necessary to understand that the practice of Tibetan medicine and the practice of the Buddhadharma go hand in hand. Anything said about Tibetan medicine must be understood from that perspective. In practice, Tibetan medicine is natural. It aims to energize the body and create an overall balance of its four elements and humors. It is through this balance that the body maintains health. We consider the body and mind to be interconnected, with the conductive factor between the two being the element of wind. The wind moves through the central nervous system via the blood and is linked with mind. The body is the servant of the mind, so to maintain health we must care for our mind using the same diligence with which we care for our body.

Lord Buddha gave extensive teachings on interdependence, which are exemplified by the relationship between our physical and mental habits. The mind can either be of benefit to the body or cause physical problems. We can take the emotion of anger as an example; even though anger is a mental phenomenon, it affects the physical body. If you express this nonvirtuous emotion, you reap the immediate result, which is disturbance to the humor of wind. The wind of the body expands with anger. If we become enraged, we build up heat in our body, which then negatively affects the blood. Blood originates from the liver and is circulated by the heart; therefore, anger will first hurt the liver and then damage the heart. Repeated or continuous anger can create nerve disorders and chronic physical problems as well.

Rinpoche, how can we manage our anger when it arises, particularly when it flares up quickly?

Yes, most people get caught up in anger without self-awareness. We must realize that we live in a human world and it is not perfect. Things will continually happen which disturb us—that will not change. But when we are defamed or criticized, we can make an effort to avoid the immediate response of anger. We can first pause and perhaps imagine for a moment that we are not at fault, thinking, "Oh, that person is acting like this because he has trouble in his life. I must

listen to him—draw out the truth and gain a better understanding of his situation." We can just listen and not become enmeshed. Often, if we approach a situation calmly, we can reach a resolution. It is necessary to remain calm because responding in kind with aggression will only exacerbate the problem—like throwing salt in an open wound. If we don't resort to blame, the disagreement will dissipate more quickly, but if we cannot ignore the anger, the situation will deteriorate. If we do not respond to an attack, the person will calm down. You see, it is not possible to confront a river directly. To build a barrier in the river, you must build it at an angle, so the river turns on itself. Similarly, do not confront aggression directly.

It helps to remember that people get angry because they are suffering. People are submerged in their own distress, and not knowing how to escape, they keep creating even more pain for themselves. It is a pitiful cycle. Taking the time to recognize this leads naturally to kindheartedness. And as you develop your practice in Buddhism, the intuition of emptiness will lead you to greater compassion.

In everyday life, the best method for nurturing mental health is to be content with what you have and to avoid dissatisfied thoughts. Face your problems realistically. If they can be solved, there is no reason for anxiety, depression or worry, and if the situation is hopeless, approach it with courage. Worry and anxiety will not be of any help. Identify what is profit and what is loss: if you become upset you lose, and if you stay calm you win.

You spoke about both mental and physical behavior affecting our health.
How should we regulate our physical activity?

We cannot underestimate the importance of maintaining balance in the physical body as well as the mind. To do so, be temperate in all your physical behavior. The body relies on food, so eat meals on a regular schedule, at the same time each day. It is also best to have a diet of natural foods grown without chemical fertilizers, and if you eat meat, do so only in moderation. When you eat your daily meals, consume a sensible amount; if the food is delicious, don't eat excessively, and if the food is not to your liking, don't eat too little.

Consuming too much alcohol and smoking cigarettes are injurious to health, and I think there is no need to mention how serious it is to consume other drugs. People who drink too much alcohol and those addicted to drugs lack the capacity even to take care of themselves, let alone be of any benefit to the general community.

The physical work you do should also be carried out in a regular manner. Don't overexert yourself with exercise one day and then do none the next. Your sleeping patterns also require consistency; it is best to retire and awaken at the same time each day. Generally speaking, in the Tibetan tradition, there are two categories of sleep: the sleep of a person who practices dharma, or a meditator, and that of an ordinary person, or nonmeditator. Often, when a great meditator appears to sleep, he is in samadhi. This type of sleep does not require a regular timetable. A non-meditator, however, goes into a very deep slumber without much consciousness—for someone like this, regular and adequate sleep is important.

Finally, if you do become ill, it is preferable to use natural medicines as much as possible. By that, I mean remedies like Tibetan medicines that focus on returning the body to a balanced state.

This is a very brief and simple summary of what you yourself can do to maintain good health according to Tibetan medicine. You can ask a few questions now, if you like.

Thank you, Rinpoche. It seems that many people in the industrialized countries have trouble with stress. Would you offer some advice on this subject?

Yes. In my travels abroad, I saw a great many people who suffer from stress. Some seem to enjoy this tension and even feel uncomfortable without it. But while pleasing stress can be motivational, displeasing stress is basically harmful. The harm is compounded if a person is engaged in numerous and diverse stressful activities, even if they are gratifying.

Try to remember that you end work by stopping, not by doing. When you begin projects, always seek the blessing of the Triple Gems and refrain from worrying about whether or not you will be successful. If you initiate many activities but lack focus, you won't complete them, and lack of completion causes frustration and stress. So take a realistic approach to what you can do. Check your expectations to make sure they are reasonable, given your individual circumstances.

To minimize stress, it is imperative to be satisfied with what you have, both when you practice dharma and in daily life. According to the Buddhist tradition, we should stay our wants and desires, keeping our lives simple. It is so important to develop acceptance about our lives. By acceptance, I mean minimizing our wants and making a realistic appraisal of our situation. This will free us from stress and tension.

Is there an antidote we can apply if we are already under stress?

Yes, here is an exercise that will help relieve your stress. The day begins the moment you awaken. Do not start out frantically. Instead, sit up straight, facing the west with the sun at your back and the window open, and rest the mind in openness. Then exhale all the stale air from your lungs. Inhale and exhale slowly and deeply so that you initiate the day with fresh, clean air. Do this exercise three times, then rest your mind for a short while. In this way, you will establish the habit of starting your morning from a position of calm that will then persist throughout the day. It will prevent a pattern of tension from forming and will create a habit of relaxation instead. Soon this tendency will build upon itself, and you will learn to be consistently calm. It is beneficial to do this exercise at noon, facing north, and in the evening, facing east, but we particularly emphasize the morning session because then you are said to have a calm mind throughout your day.

Would it be correct to say that when we are meditating, the connection of the body and mind is more balanced?

Yes, that's it, and here you are expelling the old stale air from the body and inviting fresh air in, which will make your mind very clear.

And should we be sitting in meditation posture?

Yes, it is good if you maintain a straight, upright position if possible. If your body is upright, then your channels will also be straight and the flow of the wind energy will not deviate from the proper course. If the flow of the wind energy is unobstructed, your mind will be clear and tranquil.

Peace and tranquility are valued in all religions. The presence of tranquility merely indicates a lack of disturbance. If you are tranquil, then you will not be troubled by problems that arise. Meditation brings peace and harmony to our own being, allowing us to bring peace and harmony to others. Tranquility has radiance; that radiance is happiness. When we maintain an inner calm, we speak smoothly and the body moves smoothly. Positive subtle habits will form, and subtle habits are what we take with us into the next lifetime. This is why we must work at developing tranquility.

I hope this short explanation will be helpful. I should end by saying that, ultimately, practicing and following the instructions given in the higher vehicles such as Mahamudra and Dzogchen is the most excellent and profound method of keeping good mental health and balance.

KATHOK SITU RINPOCHE

Meeting
KATHOK SITU RINPOCHE

The autumn months are some of the most beautiful in Kathmandu. The monsoon has spent itself in the valley, leaving the many terraces of rice a verdant green. The Himalayas are vivid and unrepentant under their new burden of snow. Migrant dust from the lowlands has been washed away, cleaning the chill air. On a morning like this, I set out with Penzom Lama and her family to meet Situ Rinpoche. There was an undercurrent of excitement, an elated anticipation as we crowded together in their jeep. We were gathering to sponsor the painting of Swayambunath (self-arisen) Stupa, one of Buddhism's holiest sites.

It is written that long ago, when the Kathmandu Valley was covered in water and known as the "Place of Nagas," a crystal stupa filled with relics of Namzig Buddha manifested spontaneously in the center of the lake, bringing inconceivable blessings to the earth. Later, Lord Manjushri rent the mountain range with his wisdom sword, draining the valley of water and revealing the stupa. The larger stupa that now stands was built over the original one to protect the sacred relics. Beautifying the exterior of this stupa is a way of accumulating great merit.

The temple of Swayambu is set high on a hill overlooking the Kathmandu Valley, its white dome crowned with a golden façade and spire from which the painted eyes of Buddha are ever watchful over the four directions. Arriving at the base of the hill, we looked up to see the stupa with its streaming prayer flags still masked by morning mist. A mile-long length of steps curves its way up to the temple; their stone surface bears the weight of thousands of pilgrims each year. As we climbed into the clouds above, we passed scores of "mani stones" carved and painted with the ancient Sanskrit mantra *Om mani padme hung*. Tribes of monkeys, which have given Swayambu the second name of "Monkey Temple," darted out from the trees as we walked, chattering boldly and holding out tiny wrinkled paws in hopes of being fed. Many incautious visitors have brought offerings of food to the temple, only to have them whisked away when one of the furry creatures landed on their shoulder. The larger monkeys find an unattended handbag just as intriguing, so Penzom kept reminding me to hold my purse close to my chest.

At the top of the hill, we greeted Situ Rinpoche with kataks and circumambulated the stupa in his wake. This was my first meeting with Rinpoche. We spun the prayer wheels set into the outer walls of the stupa, their bases smooth and worn from the touch of millions of fingers. Our whispered prayers were washed into the air by the constant tolling of prayer bells.

Situ Rinpoche stopped at the vats of whitewash, chanting prayers and adding blessed substances to the milky paint. Then Nepalese workers dressed in worn cotton too thin for the early morning air clambered barefoot up the sloping sides of the stupa, throwing buckets of whitewash in arcs that sparkled in the emerging sunlight. White drops of paint and mist were layered on the dome like a light coat of new snow; saffron, mustard oil and turmeric were mixed and whirled across the stupa to mimic the petals of a lotus.

As we watched, Situ Rinpoche and his attendant settled themselves on the damp ground and performed a smoke puja, an offering ceremony done to purify and dispel obstacles. Fresh rainbows of prayer flags were hung to release their blessings into the wind. Penzom's daughters and I made our way to a shrine room glowing with rows of butter lamps, stepping cautiously across the concrete floor slippery with layers of butter. A stern and silent monk gestured with soot-blackened hands, asking, "How many?" then gave us incense to light the greasy wicks. The girls offered 108 lamps, in sweet voices chanting auspicious prayers and dedicating the merit to all beings.

After that day at Swayambu, I began to visit Situ Rinpoche during each trip to Nepal. From the beginning, it was impossible not to notice his conspicuous generosity and sincere kindness. Being near him always feels like being in the warmth of the sun after a long winter. Last year, I asked him if he would speak about Guru Rinpoche for this book. He kindly agreed to do so and in his small room in Pharping gave the teaching that follows. Then, to end the teaching with the auspicious words of Padmasambhava, in his precise and cultured English, Situ Rinpoche recited the parting lament of Lady Yeshe Tsogyal and Guru Rinpoche's comforting, prophetic answer.

KATHOK SITU RINPOCHE

Guru Rinpoche and Yeshe Tsogyal

When I came to the dharma, the first thing Kyabje Dudjom Rinpoche
said to me was "Pray to Guru Rinpoche." Now this book is nearly finished,
and there is yet to be an account of Guru Rinpoche and Yeshe Tsogyal.
Would you please speak about them here, particularly for those new to the dharma?

YES, YES. BECAUSE OF GURU RINPOCHE'S INCOMPARABLE COMPASSION AND WISDOM, he is known as the second Buddha. He made a special commitment to liberate beings of our degenerate age and is actually the embodiment of all the buddhas. For a Nyingmapa, it is necessary to have some knowledge of Guru Rinpoche.

It seems that Guru Rinpoche is referred to by more than one name.

Yes, he is also known as Padmasambhava, but his manifestations can be further explained like this: in the sphere of dharmakaya, he is an emanation of Amitabha, the Buddha of Infinite Light. In the sphere of sambhogakaya, he is Avalokiteshvara, the Buddha of Compassion. In his nirmanakaya manifestation, he spontaneously appeared as an eight-year-old child in the center of a lotus on Sindhu Lake in northwest Oddiyana, between what is now Pakistan and Afghanistan. There he was discovered by King Indrabodhi, who had for years recited prayers and supplications and made offerings in hopes of having a son. It is said that when the king saw the child, he spoke these words:

> "Little boy-child, who is your father and who is your mother?
> What is your caste and what is your country?
> What food do you live on and what is your purpose here?"

The boy replied:

> "My father is the wisdom of spontaneous awareness.
> My mother is the Ever-Excellent Lady, the space of all things.
> I belong to the caste of indivisible space and awareness.
> I have taken the unborn dharmadhatu as my homeland.
> I sustain myself by consuming the concepts of duality.
> My purpose is the act of killing disturbing emotions."

King Indrabodhi recognized the child as a miraculous being and decided to raise him as his own son, the Prince of Oddiyana. On the journey back to the palace, wherever the child was set down, a lotus miraculously appeared. The boy became known as "Padmasambhava" ("Padma" meaning "lotus" and "sambhava" meaning "to be born from").

As the prince grew older, he realized that as long as he remained ensconced in a palace, he could not benefit all beings, so he abdicated his rule. He traveled throughout India, studying with all the great masters of the time in order to inspire the confidence of other beings. Padmasambhava's ultimate realization was beyond compare.

At Maratika with his Indian consort Mandarava, he obtained the immortal vajra-like body. In Yangleshö Cave in Nepal, he attained the sublime siddhi of Mahamudra. Later, accepting King Trisong Deutsen's invitation, he journeyed to Tibet. With his compassion, wisdom and supernatural powers, Padmasambhava subdued the evil influences and obstacles that were afflicting the kingdom. Through his great realization, he illuminated all of Tibet with the light of the Buddhadharma. He brought the Secret Mantra teachings to Tibet and established the Buddhist canons of study, teaching and meditation practices. His twenty-five main disciples accomplished siddhi, and eighty meditation practitioners attained rainbow body. For fifty-four years, Guru Rinpoche remained in the snow mountains; the doctrine of truth thus rose like the sun throughout Tibet.

How should we think of Guru Rinpoche and receive his blessings?

You see, it is only because of Guru Rinpoche's deep kindness and wisdom that we are able to encounter the precious teachings of Buddha during this dark age in which we live. It is said he dwells in the Copper-Colored Mountain buddhafield at present and will come in countless manifestations to help all sentient beings until the cessation of samsara. As followers, we can receive Guru Rinpoche's blessings by generating true devotion toward him and by practicing his precious teachings, which are still with the great masters of our generation. If you have strong natural faith in Guru Rinpoche, then your karmic connection with him is very special. But you can also develop this same faith over time by contemplating the fathomless qualities of Guru Rinpoche and praying to him.

Thank you, Rinpoche. Can you speak about Yeshe Tsogyal as well?

Yes, of course. Yeshe Tsogyal is the wisdom consort of Guru Rinpoche. In the dharmakaya, the true essence of all phenomena, she is Samantabhadri. In the sambhogakaya, she is the wisdom form of Vajravarahi. In the nirmanakaya, she is the Princess Kharchen of Tibet who in her youth renounced the dreamlike delusion of samsara and rigorously practiced the holy dharma. She later became the consort of Guru Rinpoche and holds the heart essence of all his teachings.

Most of the teachings of the Nyingma tradition originated from Guru Rinpoche and Yeshe Tsogyal. The kama cycles are the Buddha's original teachings, which have been passed on without hindrance in an unbroken lineage of teachers and disciples through the present time. The terma cycles are holy teachings hidden by Guru Rinpoche and other saints. Guru Rinpoche knew that times would become progressively darker and that these teachings would be needed in the future, so treasure teachings were hidden along with a prophecy as to whom, when and how they would be revealed in future times. Even now, they are always revealed at the appropriate time and place. Often they are concealed in the earth, written in gold or lapis; some are hidden in the sky and are revealed to a terton in meditation or in dreams.

Yeshe Tsogyal possessed perfect recall, and it was she who compiled the majority of Padmasambhava's teachings. So as you can see, Yeshe Tsogyal is an extremely important figure in our Nyingma lineage.

This is a condensed account of our precious Guru Rinpoche and Yeshe Tsogyal. Many detailed histories of Guru Rinpoche's life have been published, which you should be able to find with ease. There is a beautiful excerpt from *The History of Yeshe Tsogyal* written by Terton Tag Shampa, which can be included here. May this be of benefit.

"In the year of the monkey, Yeshe Tsogyal accompanied Guru Rinpoche to Dubtzer, where he gave his final teachings and advice to the Tibetan people. Before Guru Rinpoche mounted a magnificent horse and departed on the rays of the sun for the southwest island of Ngayab, Tsogyal prostrated to him and melodiously spoke these words of pure devotion:

"*Kyema kyihud,* Urgyen Lord,
 Now here, in a moment gone,
 Birth and death—is this not the impermanent?
 What is the way to stand against birth and death?

"*Kyema kyihud,* Urgyen Lord,
 In days gone by we have been inseparable.
 Now we are about to part.
 Is this not what is called coming together and going apart?
 What is the way to keep friendship with no separation?

"*Kyema kyihud*, Urgyen Lord,

In days gone by, all Tibet was covered with the Guru.

Now all that remains are the traces of your presence.

Isn't this what is called impermanence?

What is the way to prevent the winds of karma?

"*Kyema kyihud,* Urgyen Lord,

In days gone by, with your instructions you took care of Tibet.

Now these words are but memories to our ears.

Isn't this what is called change?

What is the way to prevent this change?

"*Kyema kyihud,* Urgyen Lord,

I have remained with you inseparable until now.

This woman left behind with unfortunate karma,

Whom can she turn to for blessing and initiation?

"*Kyema kyihud,* Urgyen Lord,

Although you have given me profound teachings,

Now you are off to the sky, leaving me, this most unfortunate woman.

To whom can she now turn to dispel obstacles and doubt?

"*Kyema kyihud,* Compassionate Lord,

Once more I request of you to never take your gaze

Of compassion from me and forever look upon Tibet with your blessing eyes."

Thus she spoke, tossing thirteen handfuls of powdered gold on the Guru's body,

Offering to him and lamenting his departure.

Then from a distance of two arm-lengths, Guru Rinpoche answered her.

As he sat upon the rays of the sun, He spoke these words:

"*Kyema*, listen girl, Lake of Noble Qualities.

Pema Jungnay leaves to subdue the savage rakshas.

The most excellent expression, the perfected embodiment of the three kayas,

Cannot be compared to the froth worldly beings scatter in all directions.

If you fear birth and death, persevere with the dharma.

Perfect the practice of the nerve, veins and airs of kye dzog,

There is no other way to prevent birth and death.

"*Kyema,* devoted Woman of Virtue,
 Padmasambhava leaves to help beings.
 Delusion covers all beings in all places.
 It cannot be compared to the compassion pervading everywhere equally.

"The way to never separate from friends is to practice guru yoga.
 When all appearances arise purely as manifestations of the Guru,
 This and no other is the teaching that prevents separation.

"*Kyema,* listen girl, Consort of Vast Space.
 Padmasambhava is going to the light of the lotus
 Upon the request of the buddhas, past, present and future.
 This departure cannot be compared to the flight of beings pursued by the Lord of Death.
 You have attained siddhi in this noble female body.
 Ask for initiation, empowerment and blessing from the lord, mind itself.
 There is no regent of Guru Padma other than that.

"*Kyema,* Yeshe Tsogyalma,
 Padmasambhava is leaving for the place of Great Bliss.
 This deity, eternal and inherent within the dharmakaya
 Cannot be compared to those beings separated in mind and body.
 The profound instructions are enough to liberate oneself.

"The way to liberate oneself from form body is to meditate on Mahasandhi.
 To dispel obstacles and increase siddhi, pray and rest in samadhi.
 There is no better way to extinguish all obstruction
 Than this blessing of the Guru.

"*Kyema,* listen woman, Sky-Blue Shining One.
 Many instructions have been given in days gone by,
 And precisely the essence is this:
 Meditate on guru yoga.
 This is the way to dispel all doubts and difficulties.

"On the crown of one's head is a lotus where rests
A moon on which Padmasambhava, the Guru of all beings, abides.
Surrounded by rainbow light, he has one face and two hands, holding dorje and benda.
Clad in his secret robes, with the sacred red cloth wrapped about him.
Wearing an eagle feather upon his crown and earrings in his ears,
He symbolically expounds on the teachings of all the yanas.

"In lotus posture and radiant with light, the Guru sits with ease,
Blazing with light, possessor of extraordinary signs.
He is surrounded by many dakinis.
Meditate until the Guru appears vividly in your mind with five rainbow colors shimmering.
Rest in samadhi, receiving his initiations.
Recite the Guru mantra, the essence of essence.
Ultimately, the body, speech and mind of the Guru and disciple,
The meditator and the meditation are experienced as inseparable.

"Pray and dedicate to your guru.
Rest in the great bindu of Mahasandhi free of all bonds.
There is no teacher superior to that, Lady Tsogyal.
The compassion of Padmasambhava has no east or west.
The thread of compassion's light can never be broken in this land of Tibet.

"Padmasambhava remains before his children who pray to him,
And there will be no parting or meeting.
For those devoted, the Guru remains.
From those with wrong views, the Guru will remain hidden.
Even then, the Guru is inherent within them.

"Devoted sons and daughters are protected by compassion forever.
Hence, always on the tenth day of the rising moon
And on the tenth day of the waning moon,
Padmasambhava will visit.

"Upon the rays of the sun, I will come,
Manifesting four different emanations during the four times.
Accordingly, siddhi will be bestowed,
And on the twenty-fifth day, the powerful and wrathful will be accomplished.

"The Guru will visit on the fifteenth day.
  He will come on the rays of the moon.
  By the compassion and blessing of the Guru, samsara's very roots will be shaken.
  Even the lower realms will be emptied.
  Power and activity will bring accomplishment for all beings.

"Upon each eighth day, the Guru will visit
  In the morning before sunrise and in the evening after sunset.
  Riding on a horse, Changshe,
  The Guru will wander through every corner of the world,
  Bestowing all siddhis.

"The wheel of the dharma will be turned in the land of savages
  For the beings of the twenty-one and thirty islands
  Where no sounds of dharma have been uttered.

"By emanating one hundred thousand different forms—
  Fire, water, air, space, sky, rainbow, sound and earth—
  By peaceful, increasing, powerful and wrathful means,
  I go with equanimity to lead the savage island dwellers into great bliss.

"For the next hundred years and more,
  You girl, work for the welfare of the Tibetan people.
  When you reach the age of one hundred and one, go to the island of Ngayab Ling.
  There, you and I, Padmasambhava, will work together for sentient beings.

"There, you will be the lady, with the name of Rigdzin Ting Od Barma.
  The winds of karma, birth and death will be annihilated
  As long as body, speech and mind remain with me.

"In the future, many emanations will come for the welfare of sentient beings.
  This continuity will never be broken in the land of Tibet.
  While working for beings, do not be concerned about worry or hardship.

"Therefore, now, Tsogyalma, be in samadhi.
  Although for the time being it seems we part,
  You and I shall never part, even for a moment."

Words of Thanks

The great number of people who have given their support to this book is heartwarming. Without their benevolence and generosity, the project could not have been completed. First and foremost, we express our reverence and deepest gratitude to the masters whose words and images were so kindly and freely offered for the pages of this book.

For their immense generosity, we extend our sincere appreciation to the sponsors of this project: Hanneka Pelincke, Jeff Miller and Maile Wall, Andrew and Pamela Johnston, Nai-Chu Ding, Craig Maas, David Santen, Rose Finney, Sally Bell, Janis Batchelder, James Kalfas, Anne Meehan, Christine Longacre and Paul DeJong, Manoel Vidal and Sonam Tsomo Gottlieb.

We also thank the excellent Buddhist scholars who patiently translated and clarified certain passages: the Padmakara Translation Committee, Lama Tharchin Rinpoche, Matthieu Ricard, Hugh Thompson, Lama Lobsang Drakpa, Richard Barron, John Canti, Penzom Lama, Semo Sonam Palmo, Lama Tsering Everest, Teinlay Palsang Trogawa, Claude Herail, as well as Tulku Thubten Rinpoche, for translating "My Vital Advice," taken from *The Collected Works of Jamyang Khyentse Chökyi Lodrö*.

Special appreciation is due Lama Drimed Norbu, Spiritual Director of Chagdud Gonpa in North America, and all those at Padma Publishing and Rigdzin Ling for encouraging creative freedom. Kim McLaughlin brought ease to the process with her constant guidance and humor. With her incredible attention to detail and altruistic work ethic, Gina Tesser Phelan managed to weave the many threads involved in production into a coherent fabric. Kathryn Gessner's encouragement, support and editorial suggestions were indispensable. Special thanks go to Antonia Miano, Peg Michie and Jennifer Jacobs, who gave selflessly of their hours, days and weeks. Pat Barrodale, Cheryl Burgess, Mark Rothe, Dawn McConnell, Roni Kebir, Eric Swanson, Michal Abrams and Kelly Roberts also aided the project in multifaceted ways.

Dennis Hearne's skill and patience encouraged my creative interpretation in producing the photographs and is deeply appreciated. The extreme care and aesthetic sensitivity Joseph Guglietti applied to the design of the book was extraordinary. His interpretation has enhanced the visual nature of this work.

Lama Shenpen Drolma and the sangha at Iron Knot Ranch made it possible for the royalties from Sacred Voices to be dedicated to saving lives. Their contribution is immeasurable and will continue to help innumerable beings. David Schonbrunn gave in ways too numerous to list. Kathryn Meeske would particularly like to acknowledge and thank Francis Dreher, Yin-wah Ma, Linda and Richard Page and Chris Meeske for their inexhaustible patience and vital support.

We thank the Padmakara Translation Group for permission to print their translation of "The Song of Illusion," a letter of instruction to his disciples written by Khenpo Jamyang Dorje (Nyoshul Khenpo Rinpoche) in Dordogne, France, 1981; and Shambhala Publications for permission to print the verse on page 230, from *The Lotus Born: The Life Story of Padmasambhava,* composed by Yeshe Tsogyal, revealed by Nyang Tal Nyima Oser, and translated from the Tibetan by Erik Pema Kunsang; © 1993 by Erik Hein Schmidt; reprinted by arrangement with Shambhala Publications, Inc., Boston, Massachusetts, www.shambhala.com.

Amitayus
The buddha of long life and the lord of Sukhavati, the western buddha paradise.

Atisha
Also known as Dipankara. He was the abbot of the famous Vikramasila University in India. Later in his life, he founded the Kadampa tradition in Tibet.

Avalokiteshvara
The buddha who is the essence of love and compassion.

bodhicitta
Enlightened heart, which seeks ultimate liberation for all beings equally. It is the main practice of Mahayana Buddhism.

bodhisattva
One who seeks buddhahood not merely for oneself, but for the sake of all beings, and who courageously endures all hardship in order to liberate others.

Boudhanath
A Tibetan community in the Kathmandu Valley of Nepal where the Boudhanath Stupa is located.

Boudhanath stupa
One of the two great stupas in the Kathmandu Valley. Built by four brothers who in their future lives brought the dharma to Tibet, it brings liberation to those who see it.

Buddha Shakyamuni
Born as the Indian prince Siddhartha, who renounced his kingdom to seek enlightenment. He attained awakening under the Bodhi tree in Bodhgaya and in that moment became known as Buddha Shakyamuni. In the Mahayana tradition, he is said to have been born fully enlightened.

buddhafield
A pure realm where buddhas and bodhisattvas reside, and where ordinary phenomena have been purified and so no longer exist.

Buddhadharma
See dharma.

chakra
A Sanskrit term referring to an ethereal body within the physical body. It can also be translated as "wheel" or "center." It is the vital point of energy and awareness used in tantra as the main avenue for igniting the dynamism of supreme awareness.

Changshe
A supreme, magical horse that can travel across the universe in seconds, miraculously carrying one to one's destination. It symbolizes the path of dharma, which takes one from the land of suffering to the city of nirvana.

Chokling Tersar
The revelations, or termas, of the great terton Chokgyur Dechen Lingpa, who was an emanation of Padmasambhava. They consist of guru, deva and dakini sadhanas.

Clear Light
Innate wisdom, free of all inner obscurations. It is the inherently luminous and pure all-knowing awareness that resides in all beings. The term is used in both the sutras and the tantras.

completion stage
A practice of the Nyingma tantra tradition. It is an aspect of the Tantrayana utilizing the chakras, prana and bindu (in Tibetan tsa, lung and tigle) to eradicate gross and subtle karmic propensities and to bring about luminous awareness.

Copper-Colored Mountain
Known in Tibetan as Zangdokpalri, it is the paradise where Padmasambhava resides. According to the Nyingma teachings, it is not a particular location, but one's own pure perceptions.

dakini
The Tibetan equivalent, khandroma, literally means "skydancer" or "she who dances in the space of absolute truth." This feminine form symbolizes enlightened wisdom and is one of the Three Roots of the Nyingma tradition.

development stage
A stage of meditation in the Nyingma tradition that purifies karmic propensities linked to the four ordinary kinds of birth (womb birth, egg birth, moisture birth and spontaneous birth). By seeing all forms as the deity, hearing all sound as mantra and viewing mind as wisdom, one who practices this skillful method transcends and eradicates impure perception.

dharma
The noble path of the Buddha, including the teachings and practices. Other meanings include: phenomena, path, discipline and law.

dharma wheel
The teachings of the Buddha explaining the profound meaning of the Four Noble Truths, emptiness and buddha nature.

dharmakaya
One of the three kayas. It is the pinnacle of attainment on the path, where all obscurations and their residues have vanished, and all enlightened attributes are simultaneously accomplished. It is the source of all enlightened dimensions, or kayas.

dharmapalas
The guardians who protect both the teachings and the followers of the Buddha.

dorje and benda
Ritual implements of Padmasambhava, vajra and skullcup.

Drimé Öser
An epithet of Longchen Rabjam, a prominent master of the Nyingma tradition and the author of numerous teachings crystallizing the doctrine of Dzogchen.

Dudjom Tersar
A lineage of the Nyingma tradition based on the teachings and revelations, or termas, of two extraordinary enlightened masters, Dudjom Lingpa and his incarnation, Kyabje Dudjom Rinpoche, through which many meditators and disciples have achieved supreme realization.

Dzogchen
The king of all dharma teachings according to the Nyingma tantra. It is the highest teaching of the Buddha and a direct lineage transmitted from the primordial buddha Samantabhadra. Its unique characteristic is enlightenment in a single moment through realization of one's innate luminous awareness. Dzog means "complete," as all the teachings of the Buddha are complete within this path. Chenpo means "greatest," "highest" or "most exalted."

Eight Commands
A cycle of eight practices known in Tibetan as Kagye. Five focus on wisdom deities and three on worldly gods. These are specific to the Nyingma school and were established by Padmasambhava.

eight worldly concerns
Loss and gain, pleasure and pain, praise and blame, obscurity and fame.

Ema
A Tibetan exclamation meaning "How wondrous!"

emptiness
The notion that nothing truly exists or has any inherent characteristics, that everything comes into being, dependent on various factors and components. It is not nonexistence, but rather freedom from preconceived notions.

Gesar of Ling
A famous Tibetan warrior and hero. He has two aspects: first, he plays an important role as a deity or guardian in Tibetan Buddhism, especially in the Nyingma tradition; second, he is a Tibetan historical figure and cultural hero who subdued many evil leaders and liberated the kingdom around him.

ground luminosity
Primordial awareness.

Hayagriva
A tantric deity with a horse's head extending from the crown of his head amid flaming hair. He is the wrathful aspect of Buddha Amitabha from the eight sadhana teachings of the Nyingma school.

Hinayana
The path of liberation for oneself alone, which is based on the first cycle of the Buddha's teachings.

initiation
A tantric method of purifying karmic obscurations and ripening the wisdom mind of the recipient. The purpose of initiation is to awaken to the ultimate deity, the expression of one's true nature. It is also known as empowerment.

Jewel buddha family
One of the five buddha families. It is the southern buddha family and symbolizes the transformation of pride through the skillful means of tantra into the wisdom of equanimity, one of the five wisdoms in Vajrayana Buddhism. This transformation is perfected by the lord of the Jewel family, Buddha Ratnasambhava.

kalpa
A great eon consisting of innumerable years.

kama
One of the two great systems of the Nyingma teachings. It is a collection based on both the Nyingma tantra and scholarly writings.

katak
A white silk scarf used as an offering to express one's reverence and good heart.

Khampa
A person from Kham, one of the three provinces of eastern Tibet, along with U-tsang and Amdo.

kila
Literally "dagger." It is used as a symbol in certain tantric ceremonies and is another name for the deity Vajrakilaya.

Kyabje
Literally "Lord of Refuge." It is an honorific title for supreme masters.

kye dzog
A Tibetan contraction of "kye rim" (creation yoga, or development stage practice) and "dzog rim" (completion yoga, or completion stage practice). It is the foundation of Vajrayana.

Kye Ho
A Tibetan expression used for calling out to someone.

Kyema Kyihud
A Tibetan expression meaning "alas."

lama
A Tibetan term for a qualified teacher or guru.

Mahamudra
Literally "great seal." It refers to both a body of teachings and a state of realization, an unchanging great bliss arising from realizing stainless truth, which, like the sky, can never be improved or diminished. It also refers to the lineage transmitted from the great Indian masters Tilopa and Naropa.

Mahasandhi
The Sanskrit equivalent of the Tibetan "Dzogchen."

Mahayana
The body of teachings concerning the notions of emptiness and buddha nature. It is called the "great vehicle" because it is based on the pure motivation to carry all sentient beings across the ocean of sorrow.

Mandarava
An Indian princess who renounced her royal status and became a disciple and wisdom consort of Padmasambhava. She was a great master and lineage holder of the Nyingma tradition.

Manjushri
A deity, buddha and bodhisattva; the embodiment of wisdom and knowledge. In general, deities often signify specific enlightened states of consciousness. Manjushri symbolizes transcendent knowledge, beyond words and concepts, which is the realization of emptiness or nonduality.

Maratika
A cave in Nepal, now a place of pilgrimage, where Mandarava and Padmasambhava achieved the siddhi of long life.

Nagarjuna
One of the six great Buddhist scholars who propagated the teachings of the Mahayana school in India.

Namzig Buddha
In Sanskrit, Vipashayi. He was the first buddha of the Seven Enlightened Heroes, the seven buddhas of this eon who have already appeared in this world.

Ngayab
An island paradise of Padmasambhava. Geographically, it is said to be located southwest of Tibet and India. Esoterically, it is understood to be the realm of pure consciousness where one can encounter the inner guru.

nirmanakaya
The third kaya, or body, which a buddha manifests in myriad forms and myriad ways throughout all universes in order to liberate every being. This kaya can be perceived by both sublime and ordinary beings.

nirvana
Great awakening beyond sorrow.

Oddiyana
A kingdom in the northwest of ancient India that was the birthplace of Padmasambhava.

oral transmission
Sublime teachings, beyond the scriptures, that are passed from master to disciple and are a direct transmission.

ordinary attainment
Meditation accomplishment, such as flying, mind reading, knowing the past, present and future, controlling wealth, clairvoyance, becoming invisible and healing others.

pema
Lotus.

Prahevajra
The Indian mahasiddha (known in Tibetan as Garab Dorje) who received all the cycles of Dzogchen teachings from Buddha Vajrasattva. He transmitted Dzogchen in its entirety to the human realm and achieved rainbow body in his lifetime.

prayer flags
Colorful cloth flags stamped with prayers whose blessings are carried into the environment by the element of wind. They are often strung near homes, cemeteries and mountains to dispel adversity, such as famine, war and all types of negativity.

puja
A ritual ceremony which involves prayer, meditation and offerings as a means to purify one's consciosness of inner defilements and to bring about luminous awareness.

pundarika flower
A white lotus.

rainbow body
The fruition of the meditation voyage, the peak of inner awakening. Particularly in the Nyingma lineage, many great masters have demonstrated marvelous miracles, indicating their attainment of higher realization by the dematerialization of their body at the time of death.

raksha
According to Indian literature, one who eats human flesh.

Rigpa
According to the Dzogchen teachings, the all-pervasive self-existent awareness inherent in all beings as buddha mind. It is not necessarily an exalted state of consciousness; rather, it is the nature of mind, free from all conditions.

Rinpoche
Literally "precious one." In Tibetan society, it is an honorific title expressing reverence for masters.

samadhi
Supreme meditation that takes many forms. It is a realm of consciousness in which ordinary mind has subsided with only the sheer experience of ecstasy and awareness remaining.

Samantabhadri
In Tibetan, Kuntuzangmo. The feminine primordial buddha who awakened without cause. She symbolizes emptiness and all-pervading great bliss.

samaya
A sacred precept one takes at the moment of initiation into the path of Tantra. In the different Tantric systems, there are numerous precepts; however, they are all mainly concerned with holding samadhi, luminous awareness, in each moment.

Sambhogakaya
One of the three kayas. The enlightened dimension that is transcendent and beyond the world. It can be glimpsed only on the higher levels of meditative absorption and cannot be captured by egoistic mind. It can never be injured by any outer, illusory, transient conditions, and is the highest level of blissful awareness, which makes it inexpressible.

samsara
The vicious cycle of the six realms of existence, driven by karma and suffering.

sangha
One of the Three Jewels, it comprises the community of monks and nuns or yogis and yoginis.

Secret Mantra
Synonym for Vajrayana or Tantrayana. It is a path one enters to achieve enlightenment, and is referred to as secret because it is kept from those who might not understand it or who might misuse the teachings, and thus develop misperceptions and doubt.

sentient beings
Those whose karmic propensities and ignorance of their true nature bind them and compel them to wander in samsara.

Seven-Line Prayer
The essence of all prayers, composed by Padmasambhava himself. It was discovered by many great Nyingma masters in visions and revelations and is used to invoke Padmasambhava's inconceivable blessings and initiations.

Shakya Shri
A revered Dzogchen yogi and master, renowned throughout Tibet.

Shantarakshita
The great Indian scholar and monk who came to Tibet at the request of King Trisong Deutsen, establishing the monastic order of Buddhism there.

Shantideva
The eighth-century bodhisattva, scholar and mahasiddha from Nalanda University in India who wrote *The Bodhicaryavatara* (*The Way of the Bodhisattva*).

siddhi
Spiritual attainment that results from practicing the tantric path. It is usually categorized as two types: ordinary and extraordinary. *See* sublime siddhi *and* ordinary attainment.

stupa
A sacred formation that symbolizes buddha mind. The eight known types of stupas commemorate the eight spiritual epiphanies of the Buddha's life: miraculous birth, enlightenment, turning the wheel of the dharma, performing miracles, descent from Tushita Heaven, bringing harmony to the sangha, gaining triumph over the forces of adversity and passing beyond sorrow.

sublime siddhi
The highest attainment; that is, enlightenment as the fruition of sadhana and meditation practice.

tashi delek
Tibetan expression meaning "joyful, excellent auspiciousness."

Tathagata
One who has realized the truth. It is also an epithet of the Buddha.

teachings of Maitreya
In the Mahayana tradition, profound teachings received by the great master Acharya Asanga during his direct visions of Maitreya Buddha. These include the Five Cycle Teachings, on buddha nature and emptiness, which are considered the most authoritative treatise of the Mahayana school.

terma
Sacred treasure teachings of the Vajrayana tradition, originating from Guru Padmasambhava. Because the time was not right to reveal them, the teachings were hidden by this great guru and by other saints, together with prophecies indicating when they would be revealed, by whom and in what manner. They were often concealed in the sky and are discovered by a treasure revealer (terton) in meditation or in dreams. Sometimes they are written in gold or lapis and are hidden in the earth.

terton
One who reveals termas.

thangkas
Paintings of buddhas and deities, specifically those in the Tibetan style. They are often used as sacred objects in temples and shrine rooms.

tögal
Literally "leaping over." It is one of the two main practices of Dzogchen using the ordinary senses to reveal the spontaneous, present luminous awareness within. On this path, the individual goes through four major stages. In the last, which is synonymous with buddhahood, all phenomena are exhausted and there is neither samsara nor nirvana. This realization is revealed at death, when the meditator's body dematerializes and the meditator attains the rainbow body.

tonglen
Meditation on loving kindness.

torma
A ritual object sculpted to represent deities, mandalas or other sacred images.

trekchö
One of the two main practices of Dzogchen, a way of glimpsing luminous awareness on the spot by cutting through the solidity of attachment to dualistic perception. Since its main methods are to allow meditation and to relax the ordinary mind as it is in order to experience the great awakening, this practice is known as the "path without effort."

tulku
The honorific title for the recognized reincarnation of a lama.

Tushita Heaven
One of the six heavens within the desire realm, displaying more prosperity and enjoyment than the others. It is said that beings in this heaven have the good fortune to receive the sublime, nectar-like teachings of Mahayana.

vajra brother or sister
Someone with whom one has taken Vajrayana teachings or initiations.

Vajradhara
Lord of the tantric assembly, which is the configuration of tantric deities, often represented in the form of a mandala or wheel containing a main deity and surrounding deities. The main deity signifies our true nature or pure awareness. The surrounding deities signify different states of our consciousness.

Vajrakilaya
Main deity or deva in the Nyingma lineage. Vajrakilaya symbolizes fire-like, powerful, inherent awareness that already exists in human consciousness. When that awareness is invoked, there is no need for conceptual analysis of the truth. That awareness itself burns down all inner obscurations right there, in the same way that apocalyptic fire burns down everything in an instant. Not only does it burn down karmic propensities, but it also burns down concep-

tual analysis itself, which can often be misconstrued as the doorway to liberation. That awareness is wrathful, because it destroys one's entire illusion without any mercy. Thus Vajrakilaya is an expression of that primordial inherent awareness.

Vajravarahi
A tantric dakini depicted with a pig's head on the crown of her head. She symbolizes the transformation of ignorance into wisdom.

Vajrayana Buddhism
Tantric Buddhism based on the outlook that there is a precious, indestructible, diamond-like buddha mind in all beings. Because beings are unaware of this mind, Vajrayana Buddhism applies skillful methods to purify obscurations. The main discipline is to hold a sacred outlook, viewing all phenomena as pure and perfect, just as they are.

Yamantaka
The divine destroyer of death.

yanas
The numerous spiritual vehicles that lead individuals on the path to the Great Liberation. They refer to the entire Buddhist system of philosophy, meditation and tenets.

Yangleshö Cave
A sacred place of pilgrimage in Nepal where Padmasambhava accomplished the siddhi of Vajrakilaya, thereby becoming king of all existence and subduing all negative and demonic forces.

yidam
The chosen tantric deity with whom one has a tremendous affinity. Devotion toward the yidam is used to overcome karmic bondage and, through perfect union with that deity, achieve ultimate freedom.

yogi
A tantric adept who realizes the truth as it is understood in the tantric tradition.

zen
The outer robe worn by monastics and yogins in the Buddhist tradition. It serves to remind them of their precepts, discipline and renunciation.